Addiction and
Weakness of Will

International Perspectives in Philosophy and Psychiatry

Series editors: Bill (K.W.M.) Fulford, Katherine Morris, John Z. Sadler, and Giovanni Stanghellini

Volumes in the series:

Addiction and Weakness of Will

Lubomira Radoilska

OXFORD
UNIVERSITY PRESS

UNIVERSITY PRESS

Great Clarendon Street, Oxford, OX2 6DP,
United Kingdom

Oxford University Press is a department of the University of Oxford.
It furthers the University's objective of excellence in research, scholarship,
and education by publishing worldwide. Oxford is a registered trade mark of
Oxford University Press in the UK and in certain other countries

© Oxford University Press 2013

The moral rights of the author have been asserted

First Edition published in 2013

Impression: 1

Published in the United States of America by Oxford University Press
198 Madison Avenue, New York, NY 10016, United States of America

British Library Cataloguing in Publication Data
Data available

Library of Congress Control Number: 2013949080

ISBN 978-0-19-964196-3

Printed in Great Britain by
Clays Ltd, St Ives plc

Oxford University Press makes no representation, express or implied, that the
drug dosages in this book are correct. Readers must therefore always check
the product information and clinical procedures with the most up-to-date
published product information and data sheets provided by the manufacturers
and the most recent codes of conduct and safety regulations. The authors and
the publishers do not accept responsibility or legal liability for any errors in the
text or for the misuse or misapplication of material in this work. Except where
otherwise stated, drug dosages and recommendations are for the non-pregnant
adult who is not breastfeeding.

Acknowledgments

I would like to thank the Faculty of Philosophy and wider philosophical community at the University of Cambridge for offering a welcoming and stimulating home to this project. I am particularly grateful to Jane Heal, Hallvard Lillehammer, and Matthew Kramer whose input has been invaluable. I would also like to thank K.W.M. (Bill) Fulford, the IPPP Series Editor, Martin Baum, Senior Commissioning Editor at OUP, and Charlotte Green, Senior Assistant Commissioning Editor at OUP, for their unfailing encouragement and support.

Earlier versions of the book chapters have been presented to various audiences at the Universities of Cambridge, Oxford, Bristol, Barcelona, and the Open University.

I would also like to acknowledge a Research Fellowship awarded by the Wellcome Trust, UK (Ref. 081498/Z/06/Z).

Contents

Introduction: The moral psychology of addiction and weakness of will

Mental conflict not always amounts to weakness of will. Irresistible motives not always speak of addiction. This book proposes an integrated account of what singles out these phenomena: addiction and weakness of will are both forms of secondary akrasia. By integrating these two phenomena into a classical conception of akrasia as poor resolution of an unnecessary conflict—valuing without intending while intending without valuing—the book makes an original contribution to central issues in moral psychology and philosophy of action, including the relationship between responsibility and intentional agency, and the nature and scope of moral appraisal. In particular, the proposed integrated account is grounded in a general theory of responsibility and a related model of action as actualization bringing together insights from both volitional and non-volitional conceptions, such as the intuition that it is unfair to hold a person responsible for things that are not up to her and the parity of actions and attitudes as legitimate objects of moral appraisal. Furthermore, the actualization model supports a distinctive version of the Guise of the Good thesis which links valuing and intending in terms of success in action and explains why akratic actions and their offspring—addiction and weakness of will—are necessarily less than successful yet fully responsible.

The argument on offer incorporates two background assumptions. According to the first, the question of how to conceptualize responsibility is fundamentally about the nature and scope of moral appraisal. According to the second, there is a robust, yet defeasible link between being responsible and being rightly held responsible. That is to say, to be deemed responsible for something—an action, an attitude, or a character disposition—usually means to be deemed worthy of a particular moral reaction by virtue of this thing. This reaction, however, may be suspended in light of further considerations.

The first chapter critically explores the implications that understanding responsibility in terms of voluntary control has for conceptualizing agency in the context of addiction. It is argued that this volitional conception—although supported by a strong intuition, according to which it is unfair to hold a person responsible for things that are not up to her— is unsatisfactory in general and ultimately misleading with respect to addiction. In particular, I identify and explore a disparity between actions and attitudes as objects of moral appraisal that this conception entails. I then argue that this disparity undermines the volitional account of addiction as a paradigm case of diminished responsibility. Finally, I show how this difficulty also applies to voluntary actions and omissions that should be fully responsible on the volitional view, and relate this upshot to this view's exclusive focus on negative at the expense of positive moral appraisal.

Chapter 2 looks into an alternative, non-volitional conception where the basic responsibility condition is not voluntary control but evaluative judgment. By upholding the parity of actions and attitudes as legitimate objects of moral appraisal, this non-volitional conception should be in a better position to tackle responsibility for addiction. To assess this initial hypothesis, I consider a possible challenge, which is to account for instances of responsible irrationality, such as conflicting attitudes and akratic emotions where the agent's evaluative stance isn't clear. Having concluded that the challenge cannot be addressed satisfactorily from within the non-volitional conception, I raise the hypothesis that there could be a third, more fundamental conception of responsibility that underpins the volitional and non-volitional conceptions, and integrates their respective insights. Looking at pleasure in the portraits of addiction by De Quincey and Dostoevsky, I argue that the non-volitional focus on evaluative stance is an insight worth keeping.

Could responsibility be consistently conceptualized without a notion of agential control? Chapter 3 looks into a different kind of non-volitional conception that could support an affirmative answer: a quality-of-will-based account. This account aims to ground a comprehensive theory of responsibility by reflecting on a special case of akrasia, the so-called inverse akrasia, whereby an akratic action apparently warrants positive moral appraisal in the absence of agential control. I argue that this view is mistaken. Instances of standard akrasia are consistently at odds with the notion of responsible, yet uncontrolled action. More importantly, a closer look at putative instances of inverse akrasia shows that the illusion of praiseworthiness rests on collapsing the distinction between an agent's practical and theoretical perspectives over what constitutes a good reason for action. I conclude by identifying a residual challenge, which is to clarify the nature of the relationship between strength and goodness of will.

Chapter 4 explores the relationship between two phenomena, akrasia and ordinary weakness of will. The former is defined as acting against one's better judgment, the latter as acting against one's prior intention. Drawing on my earlier work on Aristotle's philosophy of action, I argue that the classical conception of akrasia captures the more fundamental phenomenon, a primary failure of intentional agency, while ordinary weakness of will is best understood as an unsuccessful attempt to tackle akrasia, that is, a secondary failure of intentional agency which follows from and is partly explained by the primary failure that it tries to redress. By integrating ordinary weakness of will into the classical conception of akrasia, I show that there is an implicit link between strength and goodness of will even in instances where this link isn't immediately apparent.

Chapter 5 offers an integrated account of addiction and weakness of will. Like weakness of will, addiction is a secondary failure of intentional agency, which derives from akrasia. However, unlike weakness of will, addiction is a form of akrasia that becomes recalcitrant in virtue of being devoid of pleasure. Paradoxically, this is what accounts for the sense of compulsion typically associated with addiction, but not weakness of will. This integrated account is grounded in a general theory of responsibility and a related model of action as actualization bringing together insights from both volitional and non-volitional conceptions. In particular, the actualization model supports a distinctive version of the Guise of the Good thesis which links valuing and intending in terms of success in action and explains why akratic actions and their offspring—addiction and weakness of will—are necessarily less than successful yet fully responsible.

Chapter 1

Addiction and voluntary control

What is the best way to conceptualize responsibility? In this chapter, I shall critically explore one prominent answer to this question: responsibility should be conceptualized in terms of control. The volitional perspective, from which this answer derives, is supported by a strong intuition: it is unfair to hold a person responsible for things that are not up to her, viz., are not under her voluntary control. Two central categories of cases seem to be accounted for particularly well by this approach. The first is responsibility for voluntary actions and omissions. The second is diminished responsibility on grounds of diminished control. This latter category will be of particular interest as the literature on addiction tends to focus on the question of whether addiction allows for sufficient voluntary control, with some accounts inferring diminished responsibility from apparently diminished voluntary control and others arguing instead for full responsibility on the grounds that addiction does not substantially affect voluntary control.[1] The implied association between addiction and some kind of compulsion is equally significant. For it is often employed by philosophers who aim to categorically separate out addiction and weakness of will, two phenomena for which acting against one's better judgment seems to be a central feature.[2] In a nutshell, the thought is that when a person acts against her better judgment and this could be explained with reference to some degree of compulsion, viz., loss of voluntary control, this amounts to addiction, not weakness of

---

[1] See, for instance, Poland and Graham (2011), a recent anthology on addiction, most contributions to which take responsibility to be proportional to voluntary control. For further bibliographical references, see footnotes 11–15.

[2] Mele (2002) offers an excellent example of this strategy. In the following discussion, I shall use the terms "weakness of will" and "akrasia," "weak-willed" and "akratic" interchangeably; see, however, Chapter 4 where the two notions will be distinguished.

will. Alternatively, when a person acts against her better judgment and the ensuing action is free, intentional, and uncompelled,[3] this amounts to weakness of will. By contrast, philosophers who reject a robust distinction between addiction and weakness of will argue that the difference between the two is of degree only since weakness of will also involves a kind of compulsion.[4] As we shall see in the course of the present inquiry, both positions have direct implications for conceptualizing responsible agency not only in the context of addiction and weakness of will, but also in general.

There are two background assumptions. Firstly, the issue under consideration—How to conceptualize responsibility?—is fundamentally about the nature and scope of moral appraisal. Secondly, there is a robust, yet defeasible link between being responsible and being (rightly) held responsible. In other words, to be deemed responsible for something, e.g., an action, an attitude, or a character disposition usually means to be deemed worthy of a particular moral reaction by virtue of this thing. This reaction, however, may be suspended in light of further considerations.

The discussion proceeds as follows. After a concise summary of R. Jay Wallace's conception of responsibility in terms of reflective self-control, which I take to be an exemplar of the volitional perspective (Section 1.1), I identify and explore a disparity between actions and attitudes as objects of moral appraisal entailed by this account (Section 1.2). I then argue by looking into cases of addiction that the disparity at issue distorts the volitional account of excuses and exemptions, one of the central cases this account is supposed to get right (Section 1.3). The other central case, responsibility for voluntary actions and omissions, also turns out to be affected. To show this, I consider two scenarios: contempt-motivated compliance with one's obligations and violations committed out of indifference. In each scenario, we are able to account for voluntary actions and omissions as legitimate objects of negative moral appraisal only if we

---

[3] These are the defining characteristics of the so-called strict akratic action. See Mele (1987, 2012) for an extensive defense of this conception of weakness of will against alternatives.

[4] See Watson (1977, 2004) for a sustained argument in favor of this view.

abandon the disparity of actions and attitudes posited by the volitional perspective (Section 1.4). Finally (Section 1.5), I reflect on a related difficulty for this perspective, which is to account for positive, on a par with negative moral appraisal.

1.1 **Wallace on responsibility and control**

In *Responsibility and the Moral Sentiments* (1994), R. Jay Wallace aims to explain responsible agency by clarifying the conditions under which it is fair for an agent to be held responsible. In this respect, Wallace's account builds on Peter Strawson's seminal paper "Freedom and Resentment" (1962), and in particular on the suggestion that, to understand responsibility, we need to understand first reactive attitudes, such as resentment and gratitude. The responsibility conditions identified by Wallace include the following two powers of reflective self-control: first, the power to grasp and apply relevant, especially moral reasons; and second, the power to control or regulate one's behavior by the light of such reasons (1994, p. 157). The two powers are meant to replace the ability to do otherwise, which is a metaphysical condition for responsible agency.[5] This is because Wallace's volitional conception of responsibility has the ambition to lead us away from an essentially metaphysical debate about the compatibility or incompatibility of free will with determinism so that we are able to reconsider the issue of responsible agency in normative terms. Thus, in the context of Wallace's proposal, control is to be understood as a kind of normative competence, not metaphysical possibility.

Looking at the two powers by which this normative competence of control is cashed out, it becomes apparent that the volitional perspective put in place would capture well two clusters of central cases. The first is responsibility for voluntary actions and omissions, i.e., responsibility incurred for violating an obligation, which one is able to both

---

[5] See also: "To put the point in familiar Kantian terms, we may endorse the thought that Ought implies Can; in doing so, however, we must be clear that the 'can' that matters to responsibility is not the 'can' of opportunity or alternate possibility, but the 'can' of general rational power" (Wallace 1994, p. 223). Readers new to the discussion may find helpful Wallace's "Précis" (2002a) which summarizes the book's main argument.

acknowledge (first power) and act upon (second power of reflective self-control). For instance, a person would be rightly held responsible, viz., resented, for promising to attend a professional meeting and then failing to turn up without good cause or apology. This is because making a promise is unlike an agent merely stating the high probability of her taking a particular course of action. By promising to attend a meeting, she changes the normative situation: it is now right to hold her responsible for (not) attending the meeting instead of hoping that she would be able to come along. What is more, the fact that she is successful in changing the normative situation—she has generated in others the kind of expectations associated with having been made a promise—tells us that she is able to acknowledge the cluster of obligations that make up for a promise. So, with respect to promising she has the first power of reflective self-control. Similarly, it is safe to assume that she also has the second power of reflective self-control, but chooses not to use it—she cannot be bothered even to apologize.

The second cluster of central cases that Wallace's volitional conception captures well is related excuses and exemptions. In essence, diminished responsibility is accounted for in terms of diminished control. Wallace (1994, pp. 71–72) illustrates this general principle with instances of addiction, where the powers of reflective self-control are either partly affected (ground for excuse) or completely undercut (ground for exemption). In the first instance, what seems to go amiss is the second power of control, the ability to regulate one's behavior in light of relevant reasons, whose normative force one is nevertheless able to recognize, and so has a working first power of control. The thought is that people with addiction who would break into drugstores in the grips of a craving, but are otherwise respectful of property should be excused from responsibility for the damages caused to the extent that they could have not helped the offending behavior, even though they understood it to be wrong. In the second instance, both powers of control seem to be lost: not only is the offending behavior something that a person with addiction cannot help, it is not even recognized as offending. The normative competence that defines responsible agency is so undercut as to make reactive attitudes, such as resentment, inappropriate.

By reflecting on these two clusters of central cases—responsibility for voluntary actions and omissions, on the one hand, related excuses and exemptions, on the other—we are able to appreciate a strong intuition which underpins the volitional perspective: it is unfair to hold a person responsible for things that are not up to her, viz., are not under her voluntary control. This leads to a less intuitive conclusion about responsibility for attitudes. Consider the following:

> Particular states of emotion or feeling, however, are not the sorts of states that can directly be controlled by the reasons expressed in moral principles: such states as love, esteem, and goodwill are generally not states that could be produced by the belief that there are moral considerations that make them obligatory. This is why we cannot plausibly interpret moral obligations as governing the quality of peoples' will where such qualities are construed broadly, to encompass emotions and feelings quite generally.
>
> (Wallace 1994, p. 131)

On this account, since attitudes are not under direct voluntary control, it seems that they should not be considered as appropriate targets for reactive attitudes on a par with actions. Yet, the phenomenology of moral appraisal makes a strong case for considering responsibility for attitudes on a par with that for actions in spite of the fact that attitudes do not yield themselves to voluntary control in the same way as actions. How is this apparent conflict to be resolved? And what are its implications for the prospects of a comprehensive theory of responsibility in terms of control? This pair of related queries will be addressed in Section 1.2.

1.2 The disparity of actions and attitudes

To see why a disparity of actions and attitudes of the kind that flows from Wallace's volitional account is problematic, let us consider the following vignette:

> At the realization that he has been robbed of victory, Pete, a dedicated sportsman, is overwhelmed with jealousy and anger at his more successful opponent. Nevertheless, he refrains from doing anything stupid, such as shouting abuse or worse.

The case seems to prompt two very different reactions, depending on whether we focus, following Wallace, on Pete's actions or whether we also include in our appraisal the attitudes he expresses toward sport and competition in general. I shall briefly look at each of them in turn.

The first, action-centered response to the vignette goes as follows: It is harsh to blame a sportsman merely for the anger that overwhelms him at the realization that he has been robbed of victory. No matter how unsporting Pete's emotional response to failure appears to be, he still manages to avoid abusing anyone out of anger. Being a bad loser does not violate any moral norm. For, literally, Pete has done nothing wrong. Hence, it would seem unfair to hold against him the fact that he experiences unsporting emotions as long as they don't lead him to commit reprehensible actions.

It is important to note that the point about actions need not be legalistic, as it were, only registering actual consequences in the world, such as Pete not harming anyone.[6] Actions in the mind only, such as abortive choices and unfulfilled intentions, could be also included. For, according to the vignette, Pete neither attempts nor contemplates revenge. From a volitional perspective, such mental actions—say, Pete's choosing or forming the intention to punch his successful opponent on the nose— can be just as plausibly contrasted with anger and attitudes in general as actions in the world like Pete effectively punching his successful opponent on the nose. Both categories of action would be appropriate targets for moral appraisal since, unlike attitudes, they fall—at least in principle—within the remit of a person's reflective self-control. Leaving exceptions aside for the moment, to which I shall return in the subsequent discussion of excuses and exemptions, mental actions, such as forming an intention, deciding, and choosing are clearly subject to agential control in a way that emotions, such as jealousy and anger, aren't. Just as one may be reasonably expected to show self-restraint in not violating moral obligations one feels inclined to—what would be the point of moral obligation otherwise?—one may also be reasonably expected to show self-restraint in not forming the intention to violate moral obligations

---

[6] On the idea that modern moral philosophy has become inadvisably legalistic in virtue of its neglect of moral psychology, see Elizabeth Anscombe's seminal paper "Modern Moral Philosophy" (1958).

one feels inclined to. And so, as long as Pete only huffs and puffs, or even finds relief in imagining his successful opponent the victim of terrible misfortunes, but does not attempt to somehow bring these about, he would still be beyond reproach. After all, he has not given free rein to his jealousy and anger.

The second response to the vignette aims to capture an important aspect of moral appraisal, which the action-centered response is inclined to ignore. Although Pete doesn't commit any reprehensible action, he still exhibits a reprehensible attitude. The fact that he is a bad loser tells us something significant about his way of thinking about sport, competition, and, more generally, human interactions. Being unsporting, a sportsman looks like an appropriate target for negative moral appraisal, independently of whether the reprehensible attitude translates into reprehensible actions or not. In his recent book *Moral Dimensions: Permissibility, Meaning, Blame* (2008), Thomas Scanlon articulates this intuitive idea as follows (p. 193):

> For an attitude to be attributable to a person in the sense required for it to be an appropriate basis for blame or other forms of moral assessment, it is not necessary even that that attitude be under the person's control in the purely psychological sense of being responsive to his or her judgment. When something seems to me to be a reason, it is up to me to decide whether it is one. This is up to me in the sense of being a judgment that I am answerable for and can be asked to defend, but it is not, in general, up to me in the sense of being a matter of choice on my part. To have a choice whether to do A or B is to be in a position to make it the case that I do one or the other by deciding appropriately. Our decisions about reasons are not in general like this. We can choose whether to do A or B. But we decide (not choose) whether a given consideration is a good reason to do A, just as, in the realm of belief, we decide (not choose) whether a consideration is a reason to believe something.

Pamela Hieronymi sharpens further the contrast between voluntary control and responsibility for attitudes, which is implicit in Scanlon's argument. Consider, for instance, the following:

> . . . attitudes for which one is answerable—those that represent one's own take on what is true, good, or important—could not possibly be voluntary, precisely because they represent one's own take on the world. Thus, those attitudes for which one is uncontroversially responsible could not be voluntary, and so voluntariness could not be required for responsibility.
>
> (Hieronymi 2008, p. 362)

Could responsibility for attitudes really not be accommodated by a volitional conception of responsibility? For instance, might it not be the case that attitudes are indeed an appropriate target for moral appraisal to the extent that they reflect or flow from previous actions and choices? If so, attitudes would also be part of responsible agency: for they are also under our control, albeit indirectly, in virtue of being the upshot of some voluntary actions and omissions. To explore this possible line of reasoning, let us look at another vignette which, although proposed by Scanlon, seems to speak in favor of indirect control as the ultimate rationale for responsibility of attitudes. The vignette is as follows:

> Consider, for example, a man who firmly rejects racist views but who nonetheless sometimes finds himself thinking, when he sees people of a different race, that their skin colour is a reason for regarding them as inferior and preferring not to associate with them. We may suppose that when such a thought occurs to him he is appalled by it and he rejects his thoughts as mistaken and shameful. But they continue to occur nonetheless. The fact that these reactions are contrary to his considered judgment—that he "disowns them"—makes a significant difference to our assessment of this person. It changes the overall picture of what he is like. But it does not erase the relevance of these attitudes altogether. They are still attributable to him, and their occurrence is still a moral defect.
>
> (Scanlon 2008, p. 195)

As the vignette stands, negative moral appraisal might seem to be directed, in line with a volitional conception, at the man's failure to revise his racist first-order reactions so that they match his anti-racist considered judgment. As in the preceding vignette, the fact that racism does not end up affecting this man's behavior does not preclude us from thinking that responsibility here attaches to a reprehensible omission that takes place in the mind—the failure to revise one's first-order reactions in light of one's considered judgment. Thus, from a volitional perspective, negative moral appraisal would be appropriate with respect to the closet racist but not the unsporting sportsman in virtue of an important new element in Scanlon's vignette which is absent from the earlier vignette: the racist attitudes are not one-off, but "continue to occur" despite the man's apparently firm rejection of racist views. Assuming that this contrast is not the outcome of self-deception, and so the supposedly firm rejection of racist views is not merely skin-deep and motivated by the desire to see oneself in a positive light, the vignette begins to look like a clear-cut case of weakness of will that—unlike the standard cases discussed in the literature—takes place exclusively in the mind.[7] In standard instances of akrasia, negative moral appraisal is leveled at a person's failure to align her outward behavior to her considered judgment. Similarly, in Scanlon's vignette, it is leveled at a person's failure to align his first-order reactions to his considered judgment. However, unlike the standard case, in the closet racist case, the relevant failure does take place not at a specific moment in time, e.g., eating a slice of cake whilst at the same time judging that it would be better not to, but over an extended period. By articulating an appropriate timescale, the volitional conception seems able to explain what looks like direct responsibility for akratic attitudes in terms of indirect responsibility for akratic actions. Thus, although, as Wallace (1994, p. 131) points out, feelings and attitudes "are not the sorts of states that can directly be controlled by the reasons expressed in moral principles," they can be indirectly controlled via voluntary actions and omissions. From this perspective, what makes negative moral appraisal inappropriate with respect to Pete, the unsporting sportsman from our vignette, is the fact that the vignette only describes a one-off occurrence. It would be unfair to find fault with him merely for happening to feel the way he felt at this point in time, for we simply don't know whether Pete's unsporting reaction reflects a failure of his, for instance, to appreciate the spirit of sporting competition over and above the opportunity to win. By contrast, in Scanlon's vignette negative moral appraisal is appropriate for two reasons. First, there is an akratic failure to align one's first-order reactions to one's considered judgment. Second, there is also a failure to do something about it over an extended period of time. This second failure, to tackle reoccurring racist musings, is what gives the impression that resulting racist attitudes are objects of moral appraisal in their own

---

[7]   On the apparent contrast between weakness of will and self-deception, see Davidson (2004) and the critical exchange on "Motivated Irrationality" between David Pears and David Pugmire (1982). Arpaly and Schroeder (1999) offer an interesting discussion of the limitations that standard cases of weakness of will have surreptitiously imposed on some mainstream accounts. Audi (1979) brings to the fore the significance of akratic attitudes, over and above akratic actions, an analysis from which the present argument takes inspiration.

right. However, attitudes turn out to be responsible only to the extent that they originate in responsible actions.

In spite of its apparent plausibility, a volitional response along these lines is ultimately unpersuasive. This is because it fails to address the actual issue raised by attitudes as legitimate objects of moral appraisal, on a par with actions. For a sophisticated volitional conception of responsibility would be able to account for attitudes as legitimate, though secondary objects of moral appraisal dependent upon voluntary actions and omissions, the primary objects of moral appraisal.[8] In so doing, it would still remain at odds with the phenomenology of moral appraisal, which speaks in favor of the parity of actions and attitudes as objects of moral appraisal. As Angela Smith observes in her article "Responsibility for Attitudes: Activity and Passivity in Mental Life" (2005, p. 251):

> When we praise or criticize someone for an attitude it seems we are responding to something about the content of that attitude and not to facts about its origin in a person's prior voluntary choices, or to facts about its susceptibility to influence through a person's future voluntary choices. More specifically, it seems we are responding to certain judgments of the person which we take to be implicit in that attitude, judgments for which we consider her to be directly morally answerable.

1.3 Responsibility for addiction: Excuses and exemptions

As indicated earlier, Wallace's volitional conception seems to capture well two kinds of central cases: responsibility for voluntary actions and omissions and related excuses and exemptions. In Section 1.2, I argued that, with respect to the first kind of cases, this is achieved at the expense of relegating attitudes to secondary objects of moral appraisal. In this section, I will look in more detail at the second kind of case in order to see whether the assumed disparity of actions and attitudes fares better in the context of excuses and exemptions. To recap, on Wallace's view, diminished responsibility flows from diminished control. This general idea is illustrated by instances of addiction, where the powers of reflective self-control are either partly affected (ground for excuse) or

---

[8] See, for instance, Levy (2005).

completely undercut (ground for exemption). Importantly, the two powers of reflective self-control that define responsible agency—the power to grasp and apply relevant, especially moral reasons and the power to control or regulate one's behavior in light of such reasons—are meant to articulate an underlying normative competence, as opposed to the metaphysical ability to do otherwise.[9] And so the claim is that, if this normative competence is absent or considerably impaired in an agent, it would be unfair to hold her responsible for her actions; more specifically, it would be unfair to level at her moral criticism for breaching obligations that she either cannot recognize (impairment of the first power of reflective self-control), or cannot fulfill (impairment of the second power of reflective self-control).

Before turning to instances of addiction, the central cases of interest to us, let us look at two related instances of exemption discussed by Wallace. First, a political refugee should not be expected to be fluent in the language of the country where he seeks asylum. Second, a child should not be expected to become a sports champion if he lacks the physical ability required. The point made in both cases is that it would be unfair to place an agent under obligations she lacks the power to fulfill.

How persuasive are these illustrations? The worry I would like to raise here is not that they do not manage to bring home the implicit unfairness of obligations one lacks the power to fulfill, but that the two illustrations do so in virtue of not disambiguating between normative competence or control and the ability to do otherwise that this competence or control is meant to replace. To appreciate this worry, let us consider an outline of the so-called W-defense of alternative possibilities developed by David Widerker (2003, p. 63).

> When we consider someone morally blameworthy for a certain act, we do so because we believe that morally speaking he should *not* have done what he did.

---

[9] Harry Frankfurt's work on free will, in particular his papers "Alternate Possibilities and Moral Responsibility" (1969) and "Freedom of the Will and the Concept of a Person" (1971), has offered a veritable turning point in recent discussions on this topic. The critical essays in Widerker and McKenna (2003) are indicative of the richness and complexity of the ensuing debates. In the following, I shall engage directly with the second seminal paper by Frankfurt and two essays from the anthology, by Widerker (2003) and Fisher (2003), which are most relevant to the present inquiry.

This belief is essential to our moral disapproval of his behaviour. Sometimes, however, such a belief may be unreasonable, for example, in a situation in which it is clear to us that the agent could not have avoided acting as he did. To expect in that situation that the agent should not have done what he did is to expect him to have done the impossible. By implication, considering him blameworthy because he has not fulfilled this unreasonable expectation would be unreasonable.

The thrust of this argument is to show that responsible agency implies a metaphysical ability to do otherwise or as it is often referred in the literature, alternative possibilities.[10] The title *W*-defense comes from an abbreviation. For, according to Widerker, the question we should be asking when we contemplate whether to hold a person responsible for breaching an obligation, viz., frustrating an expectation of ours, is as follows: *What should this person have done instead?*

This unexpected proximity with a metaphysical take on responsible agency would be a problem for Wallace's account which, albeit volitional, relies on a normative notion of control. Yet, at this point of the argument, the difficulty raised might be seen as superficial, i.e., confined to a pair of less than fortunate examples, not affecting the notion of exemption they are meant to illustrate.

Addiction might be expected to offer a better illustration. For, on Wallace's view, addiction is often presented in terms of diminished control due to irresistible, though intermittent impulse to take a drug and, respectively, do whatever is deemed necessary to get hold of it. In this respect, addiction could be seen as incompatible, by definition, with a metaphysical ability to do otherwise, but not a normative competence, such as reflective self-control. Consider the following:

> Suppose that the impulses in question are such as to lead the agent to do things that are consistently at variance with the moral obligations we accept (say, spending his money on drugs rather than family support). If these impulses are truly irresistible, then the agent will not genuinely have the ability to control his behaviour in light of the moral obligations that the impulses led him to violate. Even if he can perfectly grasp and apply the principles that support those obligations, so that he knows that what he is doing is wrong, the irresistibility of the impulses deprives the agent of the capacity to act in conformity with them. Of course the resulting impairment of the

---

[10] A useful and concise survey can be found in the Editors' Introduction in Widerker and McKenna (2003). See also footnote 9.

powers of reflective self-control may be selective rather than total . . . But to the extent that irresistible impulses deprive the agent of those abilities, it would seem unreasonable to hold the agent morally accountable.

(Wallace 1994, pp. 170–171)

Could this prima facie persuasive account of addiction succeed in disambiguating reflective self-control and showing it to be a genuine alternative to the ability to do otherwise? The issue is of great import, both from a philosophical and a practical perspective: for the literature on addiction tends to focus on the question whether addiction allows for sufficient self-control, with some accounts inferring diminished responsibility from apparently diminished self-control and others arguing instead for full responsibility on grounds that addiction does not affect substantially self-control.[11]

Yet, certain lack of self-control seems to be acknowledged as a defining feature of addiction regardless of whether it is deemed sufficient to ground diminished responsibility or not. For instance, diminished control features prominently in the clinical descriptions of addiction offered by the two major diagnostic manuals in psychiatry: the World Health Organization's ICD-10 (1992) and the American Psychiatric Association's DSM-IV-TR (2001). According to the first, a central descriptive characteristic of the dependence syndrome (in lay terms, addiction) is the desire—often strong, sometimes overpowering—to take psychoactive drugs, alcohol, or tobacco. This sense of compulsion can be expressed in the following: difficulties controlling substance-taking behavior in terms of its onset, termination, and level of use; progressive neglect of alternative pleasures or interests, increased amount of time necessary to obtain or take the substance, or recover from its effects; and persistent substance use despite clear evidence of overtly harmful consequences, of which the user is aware.[12] According to the second, substance dependence, viz., addiction, is associated with compulsive use and the following behavioral characteristics: persistent desire and unsuccessful efforts to cut down or control substance use whilst the substance is often taken in larger amounts or over a longer period than was intended; a great

---

[11] Morse (2000) is an example of the first type of account, Foddy and Savulescu (2006) of the second.

[12] Cf. ICD-10 (1992): Disorders due to psychoactive substance use.

deal of time is spent in activities necessary to obtain or use the substance, or recover from its effects; substance use is continued despite the knowledge of having a persistent or recurrent physical or psychological problem that is likely to have been caused by the substance; and finally, important social, occupational, or recreational activities are given up or reduced as a result of substance use.[13]

Similarly, in an article titled "The 10 most important things known about addiction" Doug Sellman (2009) reflects on state-of-the-art work in neuroscience and concludes that a key element to understanding addiction is the way in which an individual's behavior becomes increasingly compulsive. The normal flexibility of human behavior, guided by neocortical "higher power," appears to become increasingly eroded toward a "dehumanised state of compulsive behaviour." More specifically, addictive behaviors appear to involve processes outside of the addict's consciousness, i.e., cues are registered and acted upon by evolutionary primitive regions of the brain before consciousness occurs. What is more, fewer than 10% of people with drug addiction, including alcohol addiction, manage to recover in the long term. Thus, as a chronic relapsing disorder, addiction has similar rates of symptom recurrence to hypertension and asthma. Sellman's account ends up with the suggestion that greater awareness of these findings would lead to more positive, humanitarian attitudes toward people with addiction in society. Here, the underlying assumption is clearly that once we appreciate that addictive behavior is outside one's voluntary control, we would no longer feel negative moral appraisal appropriate with respect to this behavior.

Finally, the sense—and reality—of compulsion associated with addiction is equally well documented in the related autobiographical literature. Recorded by two journalists and translated into English by Flatauer (1981), the experiences of Christiane Felscherinow, who started using heroin at the age of 13 in 1975 in West Berlin,[14] offer a poignant testimony to this effect:

> We went to a café in Zoo station. It really turned me off. It was the first time I had gone to Zoo station. This was a really evil station. Dossers were lying in their own

---

[13] Cf. DSM-IV-TR (2001): Substance-related disorders.

[14] On the significant role this early memoir played in defining Germany's policy on drug use as focused on therapy rather than punishment, see Harris (2012).

puke. Winos were hanging about everywhere. How was I to know then that in a couple of months I was to spend every afternoon here?

(Flatauer 1981, p. 66)

The whole terror this afternoon over a shot. It wasn't anything special, was it? This terror is there every day. I had a lucid moment. I did have lucid moments sometimes. But only on H[eroin]. When I was sober I was not responsible for my actions.[15]

(Flatauer 1981, p. 243)

With these observations in mind, let us return to the philosophical analysis of control in addiction, and in particular to the issue of whether Wallace's account of addiction succeeds in disambiguating reflective self-control and showing it to be a genuine alternative to the ability to do otherwise. To address this issue, let us briefly look at Harry Frankfurt's seminal paper "Freedom of the Will and the Concept of a Person" (1971), where addiction is also brought into the picture to illustrate the idea that responsibility does not require a metaphysical ability to do otherwise. More specifically, this ability is shown as irrelevant to the issue of responsibility to the extent that the irresistibility of addictive impulses is also irrelevant. This latter point is motivated by a discussion of the now standard, though not uncontested, distinction between a willing and an unwilling addict.[16] Neither addict could have avoided acting the way he did. However, the former, willing addict does not act against his will and so is rightly held responsible, whereas the latter, unwilling addict should be exempt from responsibility because he acts against his will.

In its own terms, Frankfurt's discussion of addiction appears to be successful: it draws a coherent picture of responsible agency and keeps the ability to do otherwise out of it. However, this is because responsibility is leveled at the two addicts' attitudes toward their respective actions, not the actions themselves. For the primary object of moral appraisal is

---

[15] Cf. Thomas De Quincey's classical memoir *Confessions of an English Opium-Eater* (1822), which also points to the surreptitious and distressing aspects of progressive loss of self-control in the process of becoming addicted. I say more about this in Chapter 2, Section 2.4.1.

[16] See, for instance, the critical essays with replies by Frankfurt in Buss and Overton (2002).

the way the addicts relate to their actions, e.g., endorsement, approval, indifference, sadness. As a result, responsibility for actions derives from responsibility for attitudes.

This is not the kind of disparity between actions and attitudes that Wallace's volitional account could safely endorse. In fact, it creates a further difficulty for the underlying notion of reflective self-control. The worry is that this normative notion of control is unstable: it either collapses into the metaphysical notion it is meant to replace, alternative possibility, or to avoid this, ceases to be a notion of control altogether and blends into a non-volitional account of responsibility centered on attitudes rather than actions.[17]

Wallace (1994 pp. 172–175) draws a distinction, which might help tackle this worry. This distinction is between two different kinds of willing addiction. The first kind is a source of irresistible, though intermittent, desires: outside these "episodes of craving," the addict's powers of reflective self-control are all in all intact. The second kind of willing addiction is not only that, but also an underlying condition that completely overwhelms the addict's powers of reflective self-control. According to Wallace, responsible agency is compatible with the first, but not second kind of addiction. This is because the first kind of addiction only disrupts the powers of reflective self-control. It still remains possible for the addict to exert indirect control over his actions even at the point of craving, if he chose to. More specifically, Wallace suggests various kinds of Ulysses arrangements that could be undertaken at times of lucidity.[18] Such arrangements would enable the addict to continue regulating his behavior in light of reasons whose normative force he acknowledges instead of capitulating faced with addictive impulses.

By contrast, the second kind of willing addiction is incompatible with responsible agency. Moral appraisal is inappropriate since the

---

[17] What such an account adds up to will be the topic of Chapter 2.

[18] I have explored Ulysses arrangements in more detail in Radoilska (2012a), where I argued that they have the potential to strengthen agential control not only with respect to actions, but also attitudes.

addict's powers of reflective self-control are systematically undercut. In the absence of basic normative competence, it becomes unfair to expect him to regulate his behavior in light of relevant reasons, for he is unable to acknowledge their relevance even outside episodes of craving.

This distinction helps avoid the unwelcome kind of disparity between actions and attitudes whereby an addict's attitudes become the primary object of moral appraisal. Unlike the original Frankfurt's case, Wallace's reinterpretation clearly places responsibility for addiction at the level of actions as opposed to attitudes. In so doing, it effectively offers an account of responsibility for addictive actions. The addict's willingness or attitude of acceptance, which is central to Frankfurt's rejection of alternative possibilities, is not significant per se for Wallace's account. The role it plays is secondary, merely to indicate the state of a willing addict's powers of reflective self-control. But if so, addiction turns out to provide an excuse or exemption only to the extent that it is partly or wholly involuntary—in the case of the unwilling addict because he can-not regulate his behavior in light of reasons he recognizes as valid and in the case of the willing addict because he does not have a will in the relevant sense.[19]

At first blush, this outcome might seem unsurprising. After all, Wallace's conception of responsibility is meant to be volitional. Yet, two worries remain unresolved. The first is that, this conception has com-prehensive ambitions: it is supposed to account for the full range of reactive attitudes constitutive of moral appraisal. By shifting the focus of moral appraisal from the addicts' attitudes toward their actions to control over these actions, the volitional account of addiction fails to account for a central case of responsibility. In Frankfurt's example, the willing addict is held responsible solely by virtue of his attitude of acquiescence toward his actions. This attitude is the ultimate object of

---

[19] In this respect, Wallace's second kind of willing addiction is not unlike Frankfurt's descrip-tion of a wanton, a creature that has only first- but no higher-order volitions, and so can act neither against, nor in accordance with, his will: for, on Frankfurt's view, will is just that, a higher-order volition. Cf. Frankfurt (1971).

moral appraisal, independently of what it tells us about the addict's prior choices or current state of powers of reflective self-control. By contrast, on Wallace's account, the addict's self-understanding turns out to be, by and large, insignificant to his moral appraisal. Responsibility for addiction essentially adds up to assessing the addict's degree of control over his addictive behavior. What is more—here is the second worry—by insisting on the priority of actions over attitudes as objects of moral appraisal, the normative notion of control advanced by Wallace seems to collapse into the metaphysical one it was meant to replace. Looking at the first, responsible kind of willing addiction, it becomes difficult to see in what respect the notion of indirect control over one's actions in episodes of craving would differ from a notion of alternative possibility applied not at the point of action, but at the point of preceding intention. In light of this analysis, it is safe to conclude that the difficulty raised at the start of the section—disambiguating reflective self-control from its metaphysical counterpart in the context of excuses and exemptions—is not superficial, but affects the very foundations of Wallace's volitional conception.[20]

1.4 Responsible actions and omissions revisited

Let us recall the reasoning behind the disparity of attitudes and actions as objects of moral appraisal, which is at the heart of the volitional perspective:

> Particular states of emotion or feeling, however, are not the sorts of states that can directly be controlled by the reasons expressed in moral principles: such states as love, esteem, and goodwill are generally not states that could be produced by the belief that there are moral considerations that make them obligatory. This is why we cannot plausibly interpret moral obligations as governing the quality of

---

[20] A possible way out of the difficulty might be to align reflective self-control with the notion of guidance control proposed by Fisher (2003). Unlike regulative control, which is counterfactual and requires alternative possibility, guidance control doesn't. It is sheer control over the performance of the actual, not alternative courses of action. I shall not pursue this line of argument further, since it is not directly relevant to the present inquiry. The point I wish to make here is that even if this move is successful so that reflective self-control is persuasively recast in terms of guidance control, it would still seem to be a primarily metaphysical rather than a normative notion.

peoples' will where such qualities are construed broadly, to encompass emotions and feelings quite generally.

(Wallace 1994, p. 131)

So far, this line of reasoning was challenged by looking into cases where responsibility is leveled directly at attitudes independently of their connection to voluntary actions or choices. To complete this critical argument, I shall now consider cases in which the volitional strategy of relegating attitudes to secondary objects of moral appraisal distorts the volitional account of responsibility for some voluntary actions and omissions, the central cases it is supposed to get right. Two categories of cases will be of particular interest. The first comprises responsible actions whose feature in common is contempt-motivated compliance with one's obligations. By ignoring the significance of the attitude expressed in such actions, the volitional conception of responsibility is bound to inappropriately exempt these from negative moral appraisal. The second category of cases relates to violations of duties committed out of indifference. By ignoring the significance of the attitude expressed in such violations, the volitional conception of responsibility is bound to either misplace the target of negative moral appraisal, and so to present them as deliberate violations, or to miss it altogether, and so to present them as blameless violations. The following comments partly draw on James Montmarquet's review of Wallace's *Responsibility and the Moral Sentiments* (2002) which raises related concerns about the exclusive focus on actions and choices. I am particularly interested in a scenario devised by Montmarquet to show that the target of negative moral appraisal is best understood as what he terms "action-for-a-certain-reason" (p. 688) rather than action *simpliciter*. This scenario can be read as a direct counterexample of the following claim advanced by Wallace (1994, p. 131):

> At least for the purposes of apportioning blame, we generally do not care so much why people comply with moral obligations to which we hold them, so long as they do comply with those obligations in fact. Thus, though I would resent someone who deliberately set out to harm me, I would not necessarily resent a person who refrained from harming me for non-moral rather than moral reasons (out of a fear of legal sanctions, say). Nevertheless, insofar as my stance is a genuinely moral one, I commit myself to the availability of reasons that support and motivate my

compliance with the obligations in question, and that could move those I hold responsible to do so as well.

The point of interest here is that for the purposes of moral appraisal, compliance with one's obligations has been firmly dissociated from its rationale. This suggestion is consistent with the disparity of actions and attitudes, which flows from a volitional conception, but is it persuasive in light of the phenomenology of moral appraisal this conception is meant to account for? To answer this question, let us now turn to a counterexample devised by Montmarquet (2002, p. 692):

> Consider a . . . tribe of cannibals (perhaps a Satanic group within the U.S.) who have access to and are susceptible of motivation by the very same kind of reason that supports our prohibition of cannibalism, but who do not choose (in a given case) to act for these reasons. Suppose further that these Satanists do refrain from an act of cannibalism, but, again, for reasons of their own (unrelated to our moral reasons). In this instance, Wallace would have to say that we have no grounds for indignation or resentment (as they have satisfied their obligation, as he conceives it). But is this plausible? If I had been a likely candidate for their dinner but then discover that they are not going to eat me—though for purely gastronomic reasons—I would admittedly be relieved. My relief, however, would be mixed with some chagrin. Evidently, they would have eaten me if they found me sufficiently tasty. Would that not be a matter of some resentment?

This counterexample points to a category of cases where an agent complies with her obligations out of contempt, not respect for the reasons that speak in favor of these obligations. Before addressing the issue of moral appraisal, let us articulate the logical form of this category of cases as it emerges from Montmarquet's vignette. In essence, the Satanists make a deliberate choice C not to commit an act of cannibalism A out of gastronomic considerations G, which can be formalized as follows: $C_G(\sim A)$. Assuming the moral grounds for the prohibition of cannibalism are self-evident and do not need spelling out, we can observe that $\sim A$ (the non-commission of an act of cannibalism) also follows from adopting a moral perspective; the latter can be—somewhat artificially, though not mendaciously—presented as a choice C not to commit acts of cannibalism A on moral grounds M, or: $C_M(\sim A)$. But taking gastronomic considerations as relevant when deciding how to treat one another is incompatible with adopting a moral stance; therefore, $C_G(\sim A)$ rejects the validity of this stance, $C_G(\sim A) = C_{-M}(\sim A)$, and by implication, contradicts choosing $\sim A$ on moral grounds: hence, $C_{-M}(\sim A) = \sim C_M(\sim A)$. So this is the logical form of contemptuous compliance: $C_{-M}(\sim A)$, choosing not to perform an act that would violate a moral obligation—but out of considerations that are incompatible with respect for morality, and in particular, with respect for the reasons that speak against the performance of this act.

With this logical form in mind, let us consider the issue of moral appraisal for contempt-motivated compliance. On a volitional view, the question we should ask is whether a relevant obligation has been violated and if so, whether complying with it was within the agent's powers of reflective self-control. That is to say, to resent the Satanists we must hold them responsible for violating a norm they are both able to acknowledge and act upon. In other words, contempt-motivated compliance is just the tip of an iceberg—at the bottom we find another obligation that has not being complied with, say, to respect human beings as persons. The voluntary violation of this latter obligation is the appropriate object of negative moral appraisal, not the contempt-motivated compliance we observe at the surface.

I believe this suggestion to be as unsatisfactory as the idea that contempt-motivated compliance should be exempt of negative moral appraisal. Both misplace the focus of moral appraisal from the attitude of contempt to a mental action: in the first case, this action is the morally reprehensible choice to treat people as potential nutrients; in the second case, this action is the morally neutral choice not to eat a fellow human being. In this respect, the logical form of contempt-motivated compliance instantiated by Montmarquet's vignette might not be entirely helpful. To see why this might be the case, let us look again at the vignette itself.

According to Montmarquet, the news that one is not going to be eaten after all, though for purely gastronomic reasons, is a good ground for relief, but also chagrin and resentment. But what are these reactive attitudes directed at? And what exactly is one entitled to begrudge the Satanists for? One thing is certain: they have not specifically set out to harm, that is, eat this person. Were he to pass the threshold of their gastronomic requirements, they would have done so, but since he doesn't, they set him free (and in all likelihood, venture to find a replacement). Quite literally, there is nothing personal in their decision to eat him or not. From within their deliberative perspective, this person is given as much weight as an apple, and a rotten one at that.

Having expanded on Montmarquet's vignette, we are now able to specify better the target of chagrin and resentment in instances of contempt-motivated compliance: a person evades harm because the prospective perpetrators do not find him or her worth harming. In terms of the vignette, the man escapes with his life because the Satanists wouldn't stoop to eat him. To anticipate a possible confusion: I am not saying that he should be resenting the Satanists for not finding him good enough to feed on. What I am saying is that the object of griev-ance in this case is the Satanists' underlying attitude—this person is only worth their consideration as a potential nutrient, not as a per-son—an attitude which is just as plain in their sparing him as unfit for gastronomic purpose as it would have been in their feasting on him. The legitimate object of negative moral appraisal is this attitude of utter contempt expressed in the Satanists' choice, not the choice itself even if, following Montmarquet, we conceptualize it as a (mental) action-for-a-reason.

For if responsibility for contempt-motivated compliance amounts to responsibility for a voluntary choice as action-for-a-reason, Wallace would be correct to point out, as he does in his reply to Montmarquet:

> . . . it is not clear that the Satanists he describes have in fact fully complied with the moral norms we accept. Granted, they have not eaten us; but their failure to take our interests and welfare into account in deliberating about what to have for dinner could itself be described as a violation of a different moral norm, of respect or consideration. So there may well be grounds for resentment in the case that are applicable in terms of my account of reactive sentiments.
>
> (Wallace 2002b, p. 715)

However, this reply still fails to tackle the root of the worry, which as suggested earlier has to do with the attitude the Satanists' choices express rather than the alternative they eventually opt for. If this attitude of con-tempt toward fellow human beings cannot be treated as a legitimate object of moral appraisal in its own right, whether it translates into a breach of a moral obligation or not, the resulting actions might also turn out to be exempt of negative moral appraisal.

Wallace does not seem to mind this upshot: as he points out in a second reply to Montmarquet, given their radical disrespect for fellow human beings, the Satanists may well be considered as "outsiders to the moral community," and therefore, not a proper target for reactive attitudes, such as resentment, though we would be entitled to find their ways "unsettling" (2002b, p. 715). This second move seems to flow from the Strawsonian background of Wallace's theory of responsibility, and in particular the distinction between reactive and objective attitudes which Strawson (1962) proposes in order to separate out resentment proper from the kind of frustration we direct at people, such as psychopaths whose harmful behavior we know to be unresponsive to normative reasons. The thought is that, in such cases, resentment proper would not merely be lost on such individuals, for they cannot grasp the point of our moral indignation. It would also be misdirected, akin to resenting a car or a computer for "letting us down." Following this line of thought, we are supposed to give up on two things. The one is to try to convince the Satanists that eating fellow human beings is reprehensible. The other is to believe that negative moral appraisal can be appropriately directed at them. For, on this view, when direct moral critique becomes obsolete, so does moral appraisal.

Yet, this correlation is not supported by the phenomenology of moral appraisal. In spite of bringing home the futility of direct moral critique, wholehearted disregard for moral considerations, such as the Satanists' from Montmarquet's vignette, does not grant exemption from negative moral appraisal. After all, the Satanists are not faulty cars or computers, but fellow human beings. The fact that they cannot even begin to appreciate the normative reasons that speak against cannibalism does affect their standing in the moral community, but not in the sense of exempting them from negative moral appraisal.[21]

---

[21] I shall not pursue this line of argument further, but would refer instead to an illuminating discussion in Shoemaker (2009). The essay explains away what looks like a conflict of reactive attitudes: most people seem inclined to hold psychopaths fully responsible for their actions and at the same time to consider them as lesser members, if not complete outsiders, of the moral community.

Having considered contempt-motivated compliance, let us now look at a related category of cases, where the volitional account gets responsibility for voluntary actions and omissions wrong, as a result of relegating attitudes to secondary objects of moral appraisal. As indicated earlier, this category comprises violations of one's obligations that occur out of indifference as opposed to malice. In this respect, violation out of indifference is like contempt-motivated compliance: in neither case does the agent set out to deliberately harm anyone in particular. This leads to a further similarity between the two categories of cases. Unless the focus of moral appraisal is placed on the attitude expressed rather than the violation or compliance by which it gets expressed, the relevant actions and omissions become either unduly exempt from negative moral appraisal or, to avoid this, get misdescribed as a different kind of guilty actions and omissions. For instance, on a volitional view, the moral appraisal of violations out of indifference would oscillate between the following two, equally unsatisfactory, poles. First, by stressing the fact that the agent does not set out to harm anyone—she just doesn't pay sufficient attention to the effects that her actions might have on third parties, and so the resulting violation of duties is unintended—the volitional account implies that this violation should be exempt from negative moral appraisal. Second, by stressing the fact that the agent fails to pay sufficient attention to the effects that her actions might have on third parties, the resulting violation of duties becomes a foreseen, if not directly intended means to achieving the agent's goals. And so, although she does not deliberately set out to harm anyone, she deliberately disregards her duties toward others. Negative moral appraisal attaches to this deliberate violation. What makes both approaches unsatisfactory is that they fail to capture the central feature which defines violation out of indifference as a distinct object of negative moral appraisal. Although unintended, it is at the same time intentional.[22] The agent doesn't decide

---

[22] The present distinction between intentional and intended actions draws on Bratman (1987, especially chapters 8 and 10), in which Bratman shows the initially plausible thesis that all intentional actions are intended, or the so-called Simple View to be a fallacy. To see why this is so, suffice to think of impulsive, i.e., unplanned intentional actions. A further example of intentional, but not intended actions becomes apparent if we consider some component

to pay no attention to third parties' legitimate expectations; it doesn't even occur to her that she should. And this is what she should be held responsible for.

Before articulating the implications of this analysis to the issue of responsibility for addiction, let us briefly consider an excerpt from H.L.A. Hart's *The Concept of Law* (1961, p. 196):

> . . . it is plain that neither the law nor the accepted morality of societies need extend their minimal protections and benefits to all within their scope, and often they have done so. In slave-owning societies the sense that the slaves are human beings, not merely objects to be used, may be lost by the dominant group, who may yet remain morally most sensitive to each other's claims and interests. Huckleberry Finn, when asked if the explosion of a steamboat had hurt anyone, replied, "No'm: killed a nigger." Aunt Sally's comment "Well it's lucky because sometimes people do get hurt" sums up a whole morality which has often pre-vailed among men. Where it does prevail, as Huck found to his cost, to extend to slaves the concerns to others which is natural between members of the dominant group may well be looked on as a grave moral offence, bringing with it all the sequelae of moral guilt.

This excerpt is especially helpful for the present analysis, for it isolates the attitude of indifference which underlies the relevant kind of violation of duties. As in cases of contempt-motivated compliance, recognizing the underlying attitude as a separate object of moral appraisal, in addition to specific actions and omissions, turns out to be crucial for the moral appraisal of these actions and omissions.

To illustrate this point, let us return to the issue of responsibility for addiction and in particular to the category of willing addiction which, according to Wallace, should ground exemption from negative moral appraisal, for it utterly undermines the addict's powers of reflective self-control to the point of inability to recognize relevant normative considerations. By restoring the parity of actions and attitudes as objects of moral appraisal, we are able to integrate the important intuition at the heart of Wallace's volitional account—that it is unfair to hold an agent responsible for things that are not up to her—whilst upholding the

---

actions, which are themselves parts of broader intentional and intended actions. Many of these component actions are such that it would be impractical for an agent to intend to perform them, e.g., they are routine and best left to instinct.

phenomenology of moral appraisal as correct to a significant degree.[23] This is because we are now in a position to articulate two irreducible loci of moral appraisal: actions and attitudes. Once we insulate willingness, the attitude of acquiescence toward one's addiction as a legitimate target for reactive attitudes in its own right, it becomes possible to draw a finer-grained picture of responsibility for related actions and omissions. For instance, to the extent that the point of action is to bring about an effect, we can agree with Wallace that voluntary control over the production of such effects is essential, if the agent is to be held responsible for these. However, if the point of action is to express the agent's attitude or evaluative stance, voluntary control over the means of expression appears to be less significant.[24] These two perspectives on responsible action are not mutually exclusive, but complementary. Many responsible actions express the agent's evaluative stance by bringing about some effect. In the case of willing addiction, this warrants a nuanced moral appraisal of related violations of duties: harmful effects that the willing addict could not help but bring about are exempt from negative moral appraisal. With respect to them the agent's responsibility is merely causal, not moral.[25] Yet, negative moral appraisal is rightly leveled at the attitude of indifference to one's obligations and the harm caused to others, which is implicit in willing addiction. As suggested by the preceding discussion, responsibility for attitudes may be appropriate regardless of how little control one has over the expression of these attitudes. By implication, violations of duties that flow from a willing addiction turn out to be legitimate objects of negative moral appraisal to the extent that they are just that— expressions of a willing addict's evaluative stance. And so, we are able to

---

[23] I shall not argue here that this strategy does not amount to naïve reliance on unchecked intuitions, but forms instead an inherent part of a rigorous philosophical method, which has been first sketched by Aristotle. For an extensive discussion of this method and its relevance to contemporary philosophy, in particular ethics, see Radoilska (2007, pp. 159–190).

[24] The distinction draws on Tamar Shapiro's work (2001), which identifies and explores three separate models of action in the context of rival normative theories. I say more about this in Chapter 5, where I outline a further, more fundamental model of responsible action: action as actualization.

[25] I say more about this distinction in Radoilska (2010), where I separate out four related categories of actions: merely caused, attributable, fully responsible, and creditable.

conclude that diminished control does not always lead to diminished responsibility, even at the level of actions.

1.5 **Positive moral appraisal**

The difficulties for a volitional conception of responsibility that were identified and explored in the earlier discussion had to do exclusively with negative moral appraisal. In this final section, I would like to draw attention to a related difficulty for this conception, that to account for positive, on a par with negative moral appraisal. To see why this is a difficulty rather than an advantage, as Wallace believes it to be, let us consider his argument for an asymmetry between these two kinds of moral appraisal:

> Holding a person responsible for an unworthy action, or regarding the person as blameworthy because of the action, goes beyond believing the person to have done something morally unworthy in that it is linked with a range of disapproving emotions that hang together as a class. . . To hold a person responsible for a worthy action, on the other hand, does not seem presumptively connected to any positive emotions in particular. Of course if people exceed our moral demands in ways that benefit us (for instance, by suffering great inconvenience to do us a good turn), we are often subject to feelings of gratitude. But gratitude is not called for in all cases where actions exceed the moral obligations we accept: consider the category of supererogatory acts that do not benefit us in any way.
>
> (Wallace 1994, p. 71)

On this view, unlike blameworthiness—the ground for negative moral appraisal—which generates the core reactive attitude of resentment, praiseworthiness—the ground for positive moral appraisal—does not seem to generate a reactive attitude of its own. Gratitude, the emotion sometimes associated with it, is effectively directed at a non-moral component of some praiseworthy actions—an unexpected and underserved advantage that these actions happen to bestow on third parties. Since what gets acknowledged here is not the positive moral quality or merit of an action, but the benefit it happens to bring, gratitude should not be treated as the positive equivalent of resentment. For resentment tracks the negative moral quality or demerit of an action regardless of whether this action happens to harm us.

Before engaging critically with this argument, I should point out in the interest of fairness that the asymmetry between negative and positive moral appraisal I find problematic is not specific to the volitional view. In fact, Scanlon, whose account of direct responsibility for attitudes seems to favor a non-volitional view, endorses virtually the same kind of asymmetry. Consider the following:

> It is common to speak of blame as a form of 'moral appraisal' or 'moral evaluation', and to speak of praise and blame as if they were positive and negative versions of the same thing: similar attitudes with opposite valences. . . if praise is the expression of a positive appraisal, it is not the opposite of blame as I interpret it. This raises the question of what the positive correlate of blame would be. This clearest example is gratitude. Gratitude is not just a positive emotion but also an awareness that one's relationship with a person has been altered by some action or attitude on that person's part. When sincerely felt, this entails having the reciprocal attitudes that this changed relationship makes appropriate.
>
> (Scanlon 2008, p. 151)

Two assumptions seem interwoven in both accounts of positive moral appraisal as secondary. The first is the idea that no praise is due for doing the right thing. For, on Wallace's view, this amounts to fulfilling one's obligations and, on Scanlon's view, to living up to others' reasonable expectations.[26] The second is that that there is no positive reactive attitude in the strict sense, the approximate counterpart of resentment being gratitude. Together, these two assumptions lead to the conclusion that only actions over and above the call of duty could possibly be praiseworthy and that only a subsection of them would appropriately generate the quasi-reactive attitude of gratitude. In addition, to be praiseworthy, these supererogatory actions should also do a good turn to someone.

I believe both assumptions to be mistaken. First, praise is due for doing the right thing. Second, there is direct counterpart to resentment and this positive reactive attitude is admiration, not gratitude. To make this point, I shall draw on some aspects of Kant's moral philosophy since it is a theoretical background shared, to some extent, by both Wallace

---

[26] This, of course, is a simplification, but not an unfair one, I trust. For a helpful critical review of Scanlon's *Moral Dimensions*, see Suikkanen (2011).

and Scanlon. In particular, I propose to consider the contrast between actions of genuine moral worth and alleged supererogatory actions, over and above the call of duty that Kant (1996a) draws in the *Critique of Practical Reason* 5:155:

> I do wish that educators would spare their pupils examples of the so-called noble (supermeritorious) actions, with which our sentimental writings so abound, and would expose them all only to the duty and to the worth that a human being can and must give himself in his own eyes by consciousness of not having transgressed it; for, whatever runs into empty wishes and longings for inaccessible perfection produces mere heroes of romance who, while they pride themselves for their feeling for extravagant greatness, release themselves in return from the observance of common and everyday obligation, which then seems to them insignificant and petty.

The point of this distinction is that admiration and cognate reactive attitudes that mark positive moral appraisal should be reserved for actions of genuine moral worth, which alleged supererogatory actions are not. For there is nothing that can better doing the right thing. To illustrate this point, Kant offers an example that he anticipates a pupil as young as 10 years old would be able to appraise correctly:

> One tells him the story of an honest man whom someone wants to induce to join the calumniators of an innocent but otherwise powerless person (say, Anne Boleyn, accused by Henry VIII of England). He is offered gain, that is, great gifts or high rank, he rejects them. This will produce mere approval and applause in the listener's soul, because it is gain. Now threats of loss begin. Among these calumniators are his best friends, who now refuse him their friendship; close relatives, who threaten to disinherit him (he is not wealthy); powerful people who can pursue and hurt him in all places and circumstances; a prince who threatens him with loss of freedom and even of life itself. But, so that the measure of suffering may be full and he may also feel the pain that only a morally good heart can feel very deeply, represent his family, threatened with extreme distress and poverty, as imploring him to yield and himself, though upright, yet not with a heart not hard or insensible either to compassion or to his own distress; represent him at a moment when he wishes that he had never lived to see the day that exposed him to such unutterable pain and yet remains firm in his resolution to be truthful without wavering or even doubting; then my young listener will be raised step by step from mere approval to admiration, from that to amazement, and finally to the greatest veneration and a lively wish that he himself could be such a man (though certainly not in such circumstances); and yet virtue is here worth so much only because it costs so much, not because it brings any profit. All the admiration, and even the endeavour

to resemble this character, here rests wholly on the purity of the moral principle, which can be clearly represented only if one removes from the incentive to action everything that people may reckon only to happiness.

(*Critique* 5:515–516)

By quoting Kant's example in full, we are able to observe two things. First, there is a wide range of positive reactive attitudes, centered round admiration. Yet, gratitude does not even come to the picture. Second, the legitimate focus of these attitudes is not a supererogatory action. The honest man only does what duty requires from him—not to join the calumniators of an innocent person. True, he does so in a circumstance of extraordinary adversity; however, the object of positive moral appraisal remains, as Kant calls it, the purity of the moral principle, the fact that the honest man never loses sight of what the relevant normative considerations are. In effect, the point of extraordinary adversity in the example is primarily pedagogic: to remove any doubt about the motives of action. It is not to indicate that the honest man has done anything over and above the call of duty.

To appreciate this latter point, let us recall another, better-known example from the *Groundwork of Metaphysics of Morals* (1996b), whereby Kant illustrates the difficulty of distinguishing between actions in conformity with duty, but performed out of ulterior, self-interested motive, and actions, which are also performed from duty:

... it certainly conforms with duty that a shopkeeper not overcharge an inexperienced customer, and where there is a good deal of trade a prudent merchant does not overcharge but keeps a fixed general price for everyone, so that a child can buy from him as well as everyone else. People are thus served honestly; but this is not nearly enough for us to believe that the merchant acted in this way from duty and basic principles of honesty; his advantage required it; it cannot be assumed here that he had, besides, an immediate inclination toward his customers, so as from love, as it were to give no one preference over another in the matter of price. Thus the action was done neither from duty nor from immediate inclination but merely for purposes of self-interest.

(*Groundwork* 4:397)

The crucial difference between actions from duty, for which admiration is due, and actions merely in conformity with duty, for which it clearly isn't, lies entirely in the agent's attitude. For admiration, the hallmark of positive moral appraisal, turns out to be appropriate only in so far as doing the right thing is indicative of the agent's respect for doing the right thing. And so, extraordinary adversity in the preceding example is there to provide an observer, who has no further means to know the agent's mind, with evidence that he refuses to join the calumniators of an innocent person for no ulterior motive but out of pure respect for the moral principle that speaks against such a course of action.

In light of these observations, it becomes apparent that treating positive on a par with negative moral appraisal does not require us to either embrace a notion of supererogatory action or acknowledge gratitude as the positive counterpart of resentment. What is more, both rejected ideas appear to flow directly from the kind of disparity between actions and attitudes as objects of moral appraisal that comes with Wallace's volitional conception of responsibility. As illustrated by Kant's discussion, the positive moral appraisal of actions hinges on our ability to respond directly to the agent's attitude toward doing her duty with a reactive attitude, such as admiration. A conceptual framework, which relegates attitudes to secondary objects of moral appraisal, is bound to also relegate positive moral appraisal to the fringes of morality.[27] Since the disparity between actions and attitudes looks like an inescapable feature of conceptualizing responsibility in terms of control, we are faced with the following question: Why not abandon control altogether and search for an alternative basic condition? This is the route I propose to explore in Chapter 2.

---

[27] Here is a possible objection: What about Scanlon's conception of responsibility, which takes attitudes to be proper objects of moral appraisal? Why does it also end up, like Wallace's volitional conception, relegating positive moral appraisal to the fringes of morality? I shall not attempt to respond to this objection here, but merely gesture toward a response, which will be motivated in the subsequent chapter. To anticipate: the explanandum has to do with the fact that Scanlon does not integrate the parity of actions and attitudes either, albeit the resulting disparity is tilted toward attitudes, not actions. This will become clear in the subsequent discussion of a related attitude-centered, non-volitional conception of responsibility—Smith's rational relations view.

Chapter 2

Addiction and rational judgment

In this chapter, I shall explore an alternative answer to the general question: What is the best way to conceptualize responsibility? By replacing voluntary control with evaluative judgment as the basic condition, this non-volitional approach seems to be in a better position to uphold the parity of actions and attitudes as legitimate objects of moral appraisal, the task at which the volitional approach proved ultimately unsuccessful. The discussion consists of four main sections. In the first, I sketch Angela Smith's rational relations view with its emphasis on responsibility for attitudes and patterns of awareness instead of choices and actions. In the second section, I consider a possible challenge to this view, which is to account for instances of responsible irrationality, such as conflicting attitudes and akratic emotions as opposed to non-responsible non-rationality, such as headaches and phobias. I then show how even central cases of responsibility, such as wholehearted attitudes, are also affected by this challenge. In the third section, I take stock of this upshot. More specifically, I critically examine a plausible explanation, according to which the deficiencies in both volitional and non-volitional approaches effectively point out that our general question is ill-conceived: responsibility is a cluster, not a unified concept, and so neither approach should be expected to tackle all occurrences satisfactorily. I argue that the partial success of both volitional and non-volitional approaches would be better accounted for by an alternative hypothesis: that there is a third, more fundamental conception of responsibility which underpins both the volitional and non-volitional conceptions and explains their apparent disagreements. In the fourth and final section, I explore two insightful portraits of addiction-centered agency from nineteenth-century European literature, De Quincey (2002) and Dostoevsky (2008), in order to clarify the distinctive contribution that a non-volitional approach could make to the current discussion, which seems to be dominated by volitional assumptions. In light of the difficulties of the rational relations view identified in Sections 2.2 and 2.3, I suggest exploring another non-volitional alternative, Nomy Arpaly's quality-of-will account.

As in Chapter 1, the discussion incorporates two background assumptions. According to the first, the issue under consideration—How to conceptualize responsibility?—is fundamentally about the nature and scope of moral appraisal. According to the second, there is a robust, yet defeasible link between being responsible and being (rightly) held responsible. That is to say, to be deemed responsible for something— an action, an attitude, or a character disposition—usually means to be deemed worthy of a particular moral reaction by virtue of this thing. This reaction, however, may be suspended in light of further considerations.

2.1 **Smith on responsibility for attitudes**

In a recent paper, "Control, Responsibility, and Moral Assessment" (2008, p. 369), Angela Smith offers a helpful summary of her account:

> . . . the particular sort of non-volitional view I seek to defend. . ., which I have elsewhere called the rational relations view, makes rational judgement rather than choice or voluntary control the base condition of moral responsibility. To say that an agent is morally responsible for something, on this view, is to say that that thing reflects her rational judgement in a way that makes it appropriate, in principle, to ask her to defend or justify it.

As this summary indicates, the rational relations view is meant to propose a general framework for conceptualizing responsibility, covering actions, omissions, attitudes, and character dispositions—the whole range of possible targets for ordinary moral appraisal. Yet, to understand the impetus behind this project, it is worth focusing on a specific set of phenomena, which are given the prominence of paradigm cases. These phenomena include various mental states that cannot be obviously linked to choice or voluntary control, but nevertheless attract the kinds of reactions we associate with holding a person morally responsible. In an earlier paper, "Responsibility for Attitudes: Activity and Passivity in Mental Life" (2005), Smith classifies the mental states at issue in two categories. The first covers attitudes, such as fear, contempt, admiration, guilt, envy, and resentment, which, although intentional, are typically spontaneous and, in this sense, involuntary (p. 254). The second comprises patterns of awareness, such as forgetting a close friend's birthday or being otherwise inattentive to other people's expectations or needs (p. 236). In both cases, a moral reaction seems to be called for; yet, neither the attitudes, nor the patterns of awareness which are the object of such a reaction appear to be under our voluntary control. For instance, we do not become fearful or resentful of someone or something because we choose or decide to be so. According to Smith, to explain this phenomenology of moral appraisal we need to replace voluntary control with an alternative, which we may call judgment-sensitivity. Thus, she argues:

> When we praise or criticize someone for an attitude it seems we are responding to something about the content of that attitude and not to facts about its origin in a person's prior voluntary choices, or to facts about its susceptibility to influence through a person's future voluntary choices. More specifically, it seems we are responding to certain judgments of the person which we take to be implicit in that attitude, judgments for which we consider her to be directly morally answerable. If this is correct, then it is a mistake to try to account for a person's responsibility for her own attitudes in terms of their connection to her prior or future voluntary choices, because that obscures the special nature of our relation to our own attitudes: we are not merely producers of our attitudes, or even guardians over them; we are, first and foremost, inhabiters of them. They are a direct reflection of what we judge to be of value, importance, or significance. I have suggested that it is in virtue of their rational connection to our evaluative judgments that they are the kinds of states for which reasons or justifications can appropriately be requested.[1]
>
> (Smith 2005, p. 251)

What seems to speak in favor of evaluative judgment as the central criterion of responsibility is the idea that reliance on voluntary control would either make attitudes and patterns of awareness morally irrelevant

---

[1] This assertion stands in direct contrast with a volitional view on attitudes as objects of moral appraisal, see especially Wallace (1994, p. 131): "Particular states of emotion or feeling, however, are not the sorts of states that can directly be controlled by the reasons expressed in moral principles: such states as love, esteem, and goodwill are generally not states that could be produced by the belief that there are moral considerations that make them obligatory. This is why we cannot plausibly interpret moral obligations as governing the quality of peoples' will where such qualities are construed broadly, to encompass emotions and feelings quite generally."

altogether or, at best, would relegate them to the margins of moral appraisal—as side effects of some deliberate choices made in the past. This, however, seems to distort the phenomena under consideration.[2] To return to the example of a person—let us call him Jim—who forgets about his friend's birthday, the worry is that a volitional account of responsibility would have to either misconstrue the friend's disappointment as grounded in the belief that at some point Jim decided to no longer care about him, or to reject his reaction as groundless. However, if we were to interpret the friend's resentment as leveled not at a hurtful choice that Jim presumably made some time ago, but at the hurtful attitude expressed in Jim's inadvertent failure to remember his birthday, we would be in a better position to account for a distinctive moral fault, which overreliance on voluntary control makes invisible. For, as the example suggests, Jim is unlikely to have deliberately chosen to offend his friend: in a way, this is what makes the attitude expressed in his forgetting all the more hurtful.

Following this line of thought, evaluative judgment might also look like a fairer criterion than voluntary control. As indicated by the preceding scenario, let us call it "Forgotten Birthday," the appeal of fleshing out Jim's moral fault in rational relations instead of volitional terms is that this does not depend on determining the content of Jim's past and present choices and intentions. As Smith points out (2005, pp. 267–268):

> In order to regard an attitude as attributable to a person, and as a legitimate basis for moral appraisal, we need not also claim that a person is responsible for becoming the sort of person who holds such an attitude. . . What matters, according to the rational relations view, is that the attitude is in principle dependent upon and sensitive to the person's evaluative judgment.

So, by presenting evaluative judgment as the main condition for responsibility, it seems possible to pin down the moral significance of both intentional attitudes and unintended patterns of awareness without having to present these either as deliberately, though perhaps indirectly chosen, or as expressive of a person's moral character or deeper self. And being

---

[2] See Chapter 1 and in particular Sections 1.3 and 1.4 for an extensive critical discussion of responsibility for attitudes as it emerges from a volitional perspective.

able to dissociate responsibility ascriptions from either alternative does look like an attractive option, if we consider, in addition to Forgotten Birthday, cases of holding adults morally responsible for objectionable attitudes into which they have been brought up since early childhood. In these latter cases the fact that reprehensible attitudes, such as racism and religious intolerance, have not been chosen looks peripheral to ordinary moral appraisal. According to Smith, this is because what we are effectively interested in is to ascertain whether these reprehensible attitudes track a person's evaluative judgments in a way that, if the judgments change in response to rational criticism, the attitudes follow suit. In particular, she writes (2005, p. 268):

> If a person continues to hold the objectionable attitude even after she has reached rational maturity, it is reasonable to attribute that attitude to her and to ask her to defend the judgements it reflects. It is worth noting here that if a person responded to such a demand by saying, "I am not responsible for my attitude—I was just raised this way," we would not feel compelled to withdraw our criticism. Citing the origin of one's attitude is irrelevant when what is in question is its justification.

This non-volitional picture of responsibility is meant to be comprehensive in two related ways. *Firstly*, evaluative judgment is supposed to replace rather than supplement voluntary control as the most fundamental responsibility condition. As Smith clarifies (2008, p. 370): "It is important to emphasize that the rational relations view and the volitional view are intended to be competing accounts of the same thing: namely, the conditions that must be met for someone to count as morally responsible for an action or an attitude." *Secondly*, the non-volitional picture is presented as covering further ground left outside on the volitional picture. This becomes clear if we consider the following:

> These features of moral appraisal—the fact that it implies something about a person's activity as a moral agent, and the fact that it addresses a justificatory demand to its target—together imply that it is appropriately directed only at features of a person that can be said to reflect her practical agency. The key question at issue between volitionalist and non-volitionalist accounts of responsibility, then, is whether a person's "practical agency" should be confined to her deliberate choices, or whether it extends more broadly to include her rational judgments and assessments quite generally.[3]

---

[3] See also: "The first thing to note is that moral criticism, unlike many other forms of negative assessment, seems to imply something about our *activity* as rational agents. To accuse

How successful is this conceptualization? The non-volitional view appears to have at least one distinctive advantage over the volitional view: it recognizes the parity of actions and attitudes as objects of moral appraisal. Once evaluative judgment replaces control as the underlying responsibility condition, an agent can be held responsible for both actions and attitudes in virtue of their rational connection to her evaluative judgments, for which justifications can be appropriately requested. What about irrational actions and conflicting attitudes? Some of them look like appropriate targets of moral appraisal, e.g., weakness of will, whilst others, e.g., phobias, don't. To distinguish between the two, a notion of control is arguably required: what makes it unfair to hold a person responsible for her phobias, but not weakness of will, seems to be that phobias are by and large uncontrollable whilst weakness of will isn't. So, either evaluative judgment is in fact a kind of voluntary control, not an alternative, or the non-volitional conception targets some lesser kind of moral appraisal, i.e., character assessment or as Gary Watson (1996) has dubbed it "aretaic appraisal." In both cases, the parity of attitudes and actions as objects of moral appraisal is lost. In the following sections, I shall expand on this challenge and critically examine some possible replies that could be made on behalf of the non-volitional view.

2.2 **Responsible irrationality**

The general problem, to which conflicting attitudes point to along with irrational actions, has the following structure. If moral appraisal is supposed to track rational agency and, more specifically, the rational links that make some actions and attitudes plausible expressions of an agent's evaluative stance, then actions and attitudes that are clearly not such expressions should be exempt from moral appraisal. Yet, actions and attitudes with no rational link to an agent's evaluative stance do

---

someone of 'selfishness,' for example, is not simply to attribute a negative quality to her (like ugliness, or lack of intelligence), but to make a claim about her agential activity. It is to claim that she has failed, either in general or in a particular instance, to give proper weight or significance to the needs and interests of others in her attitudes and actions. Moral criticism in general, I would argue, can only be directed to a person with regard to things that involve her rational agency in some way" (Smith 2008, p. 270).

not seem to form a homogenous category in this respect. For instance, some forms of irrationality, such as strict akratic actions, which are free, intentional, and uncompelled yet performed against the agent's better judgment (Mele 1987), seem to attract negative moral appraisal in virtue of their irrationality, because they diverge from the agent's evaluative stance. Scanlon's vignette of a person who rejects racism yet occasionally finds himself thinking as a racist (discussed in Chapter 1) illustrates well this kind of responsible irrationality.[4]

Another kind of responsible irrationality can be found in what we may call akratic emotions. For such emotions are at odds with the agent's considered evaluative judgment. Examples include: caring about a person one rightly considers unworthy of one's affection, distrusting people one correctly judges to be trustworthy, and failing to enjoy one's uncontested achievements.[5] Finally, attitudes might be responsible and at the same time irrational by virtue of being conflicting, ambivalent, or internally inconsistent. Catullus' Poem 85 offers a fine cameo of this kind of mental conflict:

> Odi et amo. quare id faciam, fortasse requiris?
> nescio, sed fieri sentio et excrucior.

> I hate, and love. Why do I do it, you might wonder.
> I do not know, though feel it happening, and am torn apart.[6]

---

[4] Cf. Scanlon (2008, p. 195): "Consider, for example, a man who firmly rejects racist views but who nonetheless sometimes finds himself thinking, when he sees people of a different race, that their skin colour is a reason for regarding them as inferior and preferring not to associate with them. We may suppose that when such a thought occurs to him he is appalled by it and he rejects his thoughts as mistaken and shameful. But they continue to occur nonetheless. The fact that these reactions are contrary to his considered judgment—that he 'disowns them'—makes a significant difference to our assessment of this person. It changes the overall picture of what he is like. But it does not erase the relevance of these attitudes altogether. They are still attributable to him, and their occurrence is still a moral defect."

[5] At first blush, it might seem that Scanlon's vignette should be included into the category of akratic emotions. Yet, the vignette is not a clear-cut case of akrasia involving attitudes. As argued in Chapter 1, it is best understood as akrasia involving mental actions, e.g., racist intentions formed against the agent's better judgment as opposed to racist actions in the world performed against the agent's better judgment.

[6] The translation I offer here is meant to highlight the aspects of activity and passivity in the relevant kind of mental conflict. See Catullus (1990) for an alternative translation.

In all cases—weakness of will, akratic emotions, and conflicting attitudes—we are able to observe a close association between irrationality and responsibility that belies a non-volitional conception, such as Smith's rational relations view. Yet, these instances of responsible irrationality are to be distinguished from the preceding vignette of a person who, upon reaching rational maturity, continues to share a reprehensible attitude she was brought up with, but gives in guise of justification only the answer: "I am not responsible for my attitude—I was just raised this way."[7]

In a sense, this vignette is also an instance of responsible irrationality: for the evaluative stance adopted has no rationale to speak of; it does not express a judgment of the agent's own. Nevertheless, this is a kind of irrationality, responsibility for which is well accounted for on the rational relations view: it is a failure that presupposes the person's rational agency and, as a result, falls within the scope of legitimate moral appraisal. For, as Smith explains (2005, p. 255), "rational" in "rational relations view" simply means involving our rational activity rather than reasonable in some more substantive sense. So irrationality that amounts to breakdowns of what Smith calls "normal normative connections" between evaluative judgments, on the one hand, and attitudes and actions, on the other, should not pose a problem. To the extent that these breakdowns are indicative of a person's rational agency, they are also legitimate objects of moral appraisal.

With respect to the preceding vignette, I find this line of thought persuasive. By refusing to subject to critical examination the reprehensible attitude she has been raised to share, a person "fails to give proper weight or significance to the needs and interests" of the people, to whom this attitude is prejudicial.[8] We can see that her unwillingness or even inability to articulate and defend some sort of rationale for the attitude at issue does not make it any less an expression of her rational, albeit deficient,

---

[7] Cf. Smith (2005, p. 268).

[8] Cf. Smith (2008, p. 370) quoted in footnote 4. In light of the distinction between moral and conventional norms drawn in Southwood (2011), we could say that the distinctive moral fault here is to treat all norms as merely conventional and thus exempt from the requirement for principled justification.

agency. Moreover, the fact that she refuses to take responsibility for this attitude in the sense of refusing to offer a rationale for it is an inherent part of what calls for negative moral appraisal in this case.[9]

This raises the following questions: Why not treat in a similar way the instances of responsible irrationality I pointed to earlier—weakness of will, akratic emotions, and conflicting attitudes? Could we not consider them as comparable breakdowns of the normal normative connections between evaluative judgments, on the one hand, and attitudes and actions, on the other? To address these questions, I shall focus on the third case, conflicting attitudes, where the contrast with Smith's vignette is most conspicuous. I shall then return to the two other cases, weakness of will and akratic emotions, in order to show that they also diverge from the kind of responsible irrationality that Smith's non-volitional conception is able to account for.

2.2.1 **Conflicting attitudes**

Looking at Catullus' couplet, it becomes apparent that conflicting attitudes do not easily fit on either side of the activity–passivity divide which underlies Smith's non-volitional conception of responsibility. Loving and hating the same person and for the same reasons without being able to explain why this is happening does not look like an inner failing of rational agency, on a par with the failing to provide justification for a reprehensible attitude one nevertheless sticks to. Neither does it look like the display of blind psychological forces, or a non-rational mental state, such as headache, where we find no rational agency to appraise. In other words, conflicting attitudes appear to be located at the margins of rational agency, in a blind spot for the rational relations view. For, on this view, the kind of mental conflict we are faced with here isn't comfortably presented either as responsible irrationality, or as non-responsible non-rationality. The activity aspect that speaks in favor of the former option is that there are two intentional mental states involved: loving

---

[9] The case is relevantly similar to wrongdoings out of indifference rather than malice, which were shown to pose an intractable difficulty for volitional conceptions of responsibility in Chapter 1, see in particular Section 1.4.

and hating. On the other hand, however, these two intentional states stand in direct contradiction with one another, a contradiction that is not only unwanted, but also unintelligible from a first-person perspective to the point of resembling something experienced in the capacity of a passive bystander instead of an agent (Frankfurt 1989, p. 12). This passivity aspect speaks in favor of the latter option: conflicting attitudes are instances of non-responsible non-rationality. Yet, neither option is sufficiently evidenced as to prevail over the other. To see why this so, let us explore in some detail each alternative in turn, beginning with non-responsible non-rationality.

On the rational relations view, phobias offer a clear-cut case of non-rationality which, by definition, does not engage one's responsibility since it does not engage one's rational agency. To use Smith's own an example, fear of spiders, what makes it a phobia is precisely the fact that the emotions involved are irresponsive to a person's evaluative judgment as to the threat that spiders effectively pose to her. In this respect, phobias are non-rational. Unlike instances of responsible irrationality where negative moral appraisal attaches to internal failings of rational agency, phobias fall beyond the scope of rational agency in the sense that they are more akin to headaches and allergies than to typical fear where emotion is meant to match evaluative judgment.[10]

Conflicting attitudes do not follow a similar pattern. They are not irresponsive to one's evaluative judgments: on the contrary, a constitutive feature of this perplexing phenomenon is that the link between attitudes and evaluative judgments seems to be intact; the paradox of irrationality is to be found at the heart of the agent's evaluative stance. To return to Catullus' work, the poignant expression of conflicting attitudes—love and hatred—in Poem 85 is meant to make us see how extraordinary the object of the poet's affection is; for she is able to arouse such extraordinary passions. And so we could say that the conflicting attitudes at issue

---

[10] See also Smith (2012, p. 578): "In order for something to be attributable to an agent for purposes of moral appraisal, in my view, we must show that the agent is connected to that thing in a way that makes these answerability demands intelligible. I am not morally responsible for my height, for my intelligence, or for my heartbeat, because it would make no sense that I justify these things."

encapsulate an evaluative meta-judgment, according to which the elusive object of the poet's affections is in fact worthy of wholehearted love and wholehearted hatred. If this is correct, we should aim to introduce conflicting attitudes back into the scope of responsible irrationality.

On second look, however, this alternative proves equally unsatisfactory within a rational relations view. For it would require that we hold the agent responsible for the very conflict of attitudes rather than the attitudes themselves. Smith (2012, p. 579) rejects this idea as "highly implausible" because it would imply that the inconsistent "configuration of the agent's psychic system reflects some judgment on her part about the worth or value of holding conflicting attitudes." To retain conflicting attitudes within the scope of responsible irrationality, Smith reinterprets the phenomenon as a concurrent expression of two attitudes, which happen to be contradictory. Being responsible for each attitude separately—they both flow from an evaluative judgment of the agent's own—makes this agent responsible, by implication, for the irrationality their concurrent expression adds up to.[11]

Yet, this reductionist account of responsibility for conflicting attitudes fails to do justice to the phenomenon under consideration. It explains responsibility for attitudes that happen to be conflicting but not for attitudes that are held as conflicting. Looking at Catullus' poem once more, responsibility, in so far as it is appropriate, can only attach—*pace* Smith—to the very configuration of the agent's psychic system that makes loving and, at the same time, hating from the bottom of one's heart a viable option.

We are now in a position to appreciate why this kind of responsible irrationality would pose an intractable difficulty for a rational relations view. To account for the very configuration of the agent's psychic system as possible object of moral appraisal, we are bound to either introduce a second category of lesser moral appraisal, such as "aretaic" appraisal, or

---

[11] Cf. Smith (2012, pp. 579–580): "an agent is responsible for holding each of two attitudes that, together, make it the case that she is guilty of irrationality. Her responsibility for her irrationality is, in effect, simply a consequence of the responsibility for the attitudes that together constitute her irrationality."

reintroduce voluntary control as the basic condition for moral responsibility. If we go the first way, responsibility for conflicting attitudes would amount to attributing a negative character trait to a person. This negative assessment would indeed be loosely connected to her rational agency. For instance, we could say that emotional ambivalence points to insufficient interest in the adverse consequences that not making up one's mind might have on other people.

This is a plausible account; however, it is a plausible account of derivative, not primary responsibility. For conflicting attitudes get accounted for as by-products of responsible agency, not a legitimate object of moral appraisal in their own right. Yet, being able to treat responsibility for attitudes on a par with responsibility for actions seems to be the main advantage of a non-volitional conception, such as Smith's rational relations view. If the parity of actions and attitudes as objects of moral appraisal is lost, there would be no reason to prefer this over a volitional conception. As shown in Chapter 1, the volitional conception is capable of accounting for attitudes as legitimate, though secondary objects of moral appraisal. However, this conceptualization of attitudes puts it drastically at odds with the phenomenology of moral appraisal.

If we go the second way, we end up facing a similar worry. This is because here responsibility for conflicting attitudes would amount to responsibility for the willful violation of a norm, the validity of which one not only appreciates, but also benefits from.[12] The target of negative moral appraisal would therefore be an evaluative meta-judgment in favor of inner inconsistency and, more specifically, a presumed overarching choice to disregard consistency in one's attitudes as irrelevant whilst effectively relying on others taking care to put their attitudes in order. For instance, even conflicting attitudes, such as that depicted in Catullus' Poem 85, depend upon a representation of their object as a person of a particular character. This background representation imposes a certain requirement of inner consistency to the object of conflicting attitudes, from which the subject of conflicting attitudes is apparently exempt.

---

[12] This second option closely resembles the volitional account discussed in Chapter 1. See especially Section 1.1.

The trouble with this account is not—*pace* Smith—that it is highly implausible in its conclusions, but that it has to paradoxically appeal to a more restricted conception of what counts as responsible agency than the rational relations view in order to accommodate mental conflicts at the margins of agency that, as we have seen, fall into the blind spot of this view. As in the preceding scenario, conflicting attitudes get accounted for as by-products of responsible agency, not a legitimate object of moral appraisal in their own right. In addition to losing the parity of actions and attitudes as objects of moral appraisal, however, the present scenario leads to a further disadvantage. By assimilating the evaluative meta-judgment implicit in conflicting attitudes to an overarching choice, the rational relations view would over-intellectualize moral life to the same extent as a volitional conception focused on deliberation and articulate choice. As a result, this view would be liable to miss out the same aspects of responsible agency as the volitional view, to which it aims to provide an alternative. For, as surmised earlier, evaluative judgment turns out to be a kind of voluntary control rather than a genuine alternative.

2.2.2 Implications for paradigm cases: Patterns of awareness and wholehearted attitudes

A proponent of the rational relations view might concede the point that conflicting attitudes pose an intractable difficulty for the non-volitional conception of responsibility, but argue that, since this kind of responsible irrationality is located at the very margins of rational agency, this is a fairly minor drawback. In the following, I will aim to show that the difficulty identified with respect to conflicting attitudes also applies to paradigm cases of responsibility on the rational relations view, such as patterns of awareness. To see why this is so, let us look again at Forgotten Birthday (Smith 2005, p. 236).

To recall, in this vignette a person, Jim, forgets a close friend's birthday. According to Smith, only a non-volitional conception of responsibility, such as her rational relations view, can account for Jim's inattentiveness as an appropriate target for negative moral appraisal. For, clearly, Jim has not deliberately chosen to forget his friend's birthday. Yet, in light of the previous analysis of responsibility for conflicting attitudes we might be less inclined to agree that Forgotten Birthday speaks unequivocally in favor of a non-volitional conception. If evaluative judgments relevant for moral appraisal are, as Smith (2005, p. 251) posits, "not necessarily consciously held propositional beliefs, but rather tendencies to regard certain things as having evaluative significance," Jim's inattentiveness exhibits a contradictory evaluative background that closely resembles that of conflicting attitudes. "How could you forget that it was my birthday, if you call yourself a friend of mine?," we can imagine the wronged friend remonstrating with Jim. Like the lyrical self in Catullus' Poem 85, Jim is apparently engaged in evaluative tendencies that are hard, if not impossible, to reconcile: for his inattentiveness commits him as a matter of fact to regarding his friend's feelings as significant (this is still his friend) and at the same time insignificant (Jim nevertheless forgets about his friend's birthday). By considering patterns of awareness, such as Jim's in Forgotten Birthday as legitimate objects of moral appraisal, we effectively say that Jim is rightly held responsible for the inconsistent configuration of his psychic system. And so, the intractable difficulty that affects conflicting attitudes as possible objects of moral appraisal at the margins of responsible agency also affects patterns of awareness which, on Smith's view, are at its very heart.

What's more, even wholehearted attitudes are not immune to this difficulty. By "wholehearted" I mean here attitudes that do not derive from a contradictory or inconsistent evaluative background. In this respect, they are the opposite of conflicting attitudes. Wholehearted attitudes can, but do not have to, also be reflectively endorsed by the person, who is held responsible for them. For instance, a reprehensible attitude that a person adopts unreflectively, as a result of her upbringing, counts as wholehearted on this understanding: the fact that this person is unable or unwilling to offer any rationale for the attitude at issue is immaterial. I believe that this is a fair description of Smith's earlier vignette illustrating responsible irrationality. If this is correct, even in cases of wholehearted attitudes, an agent turns out to be held responsible for the very configuration of her psychic system rather than a distinct evaluative judgment made by her. A statement, such as "I am not responsible for my attitude—I was just raised this way" does not count for a valid excuse precisely on the assumption that there is something distinctly wrong with a person taking her evaluative stance for granted. Here, the appropriate target of negative moral appraisal is not only the reprehensible attitude that this person exhibits, but also her refusal to take responsibility, that is, to account for the evaluative stance, from which her reprehensive attitude derives. In this way, we effectively include the underlying configuration of the person's psychic system within the scope of what she is directly held responsible for. Importantly, this move is unavoidable: otherwise, we would be reduced to treating statements as that given earlier as proper grounds for excuse.

By reflecting on this upshot, we are able to substantiate the following overall conclusion about evaluative judgments as focal points of moral appraisal. In all instances considered—from conflicting to wholehearted attitudes—to distinguish responsible irrationality from non-responsible non-rationality, the rational relations view has to implicitly rely on a fairly robust notion of voluntary control. This is because the apparent expression of evaluative stance either in action or attitude does not suffice to settle, but only to raise the question of whether responsible agency has taken place. As suggested by the preceding discussion, moral appraisal follows a general pattern of reflection whereby the presence or absence of rational relations between apparent expression and the evaluative stance to which it may correspond is established by settling the question of whether the expression would change if the agent were to revise her stance as a result of rational criticism. This implicit counterfactual condition of control is in fact the easiest to spot in Smith's vignette of a wholehearted, though unreflectively held prejudice. Here, the rational relations between reprehensible attitude (the apparent expression of prejudice) and evaluative judgment that seek to rationalize this prejudice (the focal point of negative moral appraisal on Smith's view) are acknowledged to obtain in virtue of the person's rational maturity. That is to say, although this person is unlikely to even contemplate revising her prejudice, to hold her responsible we need to view her as capable, but reluctant to engage in such a revision. Similarly, conflicting attitudes are attributable for the purposes of moral appraisal on the assumption that the unresolved conflicts at issue could be overcome by the person, if she were to put her mind to this task—more specifically, if she were to think more carefully which evaluative judgments of hers are rationally justifiable.[13] Following this line of thought, it becomes clear that a fully fleshed out rational relations view would cover similar areas of responsible agency to those covered by Wallace's view, which emphasizes reflective self-control. If so, the non-volitional perspective that underlies Smith's view is no longer likely to deliver a comprehensive alternative to the volitional perspective as was initially promised. What's more, the volitional perspective on responsibility begins to look inescapable and yet—in light of the analysis developed in Chapter 1—still unsatisfactory. The instability of responsible irrationality as object of moral appraisal hints precisely at that: by recasting evaluative judgment as a variety of voluntary control, we lose sight of an important feature of the phenomenon under consideration, the fact that irrational agency is experienced as perplexing, if not unintelligible from inside. Alternatively, by interpreting evaluative judgment as radically different from voluntary control, we eventually lose sight of another important feature, the fact that irrational agency is agency, after all. Either solution is unsatisfactory. In the first instance, we are able to account for responsible irrationality as legitimate object of moral appraisal by unduly rationalizing it. In the second instance, we are forced to give up on the idea of responsible irrationality. For, at a closer look, any principled difference with non-responsible non-rationality fades away.

2.3 Is responsibility best understood as a cluster concept?

In light of the preceding observations, it is worth exploring the idea that the volitional and the non-volitional accounts are effectively after

---

[13] Some readers might wonder where akratic emotions would fit. Here is a quick reply: between conflicting and wholehearted attitudes. For a more detailed account, see Chapter 4, especially Section 4.2 where akrasia—whether in action or attitude—is shown to be a mental conflict that gets resolved, albeit in a poor, unstable way. In anticipation of this account, the following can be said: being defined by a mental conflict, akratic attitudes are similar to conflicting ones; being the outcome of having somehow made up one's mind, they are also similar to wholehearted, yet unreasonable, attitudes.

separate target concepts rather than alternative conceptions of the same concept of responsibility. To do so, let us consider a recent argument proposed by David Shoemaker (2011). According to this argument, a comprehensive theory of responsibility should explain and incorporate three separate conceptions: attributability, answerability, and accountability. Furthermore, what Shoemaker terms "Scanlonian" theory of responsibility—though he mostly discusses Angela Smith's work, not Thomas Scanlon's—fails this comprehensiveness test because it conflates the first two conceptions and ignores the significance of the third. Shoemaker's argument can be broken down into the following steps.

First, a Scanlonian theory of responsibility, or Scanlonian responsibility for short, looks like a comprehensive account bringing together being responsible and being held responsible. This is because it takes the conditions rendering Φ attributable to a person for the purposes of moral appraisal to be just the conditions rendering this person answerable for Φ.[14]

Second, as it transpires on close inspection, attributability and answerability are not coextensive. To be responsible for Φ in the first sense, Φ should express a person's practical commitments: attributability is a kind of character assessment or aretaic appraisal. To be responsible for Φ in the second sense, a person should be able to cite the reasons she took to justify her Φ-ing: answerability is an assessment of this person's reasons for Φ-ing. There are two apparent cases of attributability without answerability: responsibility for irrational or conflicting attitudes, on the one hand, and on the other, emotional commitments without, or contrary to, reason. Phobias illustrate the former case. Loving a person whom one considers unworthy of love illustrates the latter case.

Third, Scanlonian blame fails to disambiguate being held responsible for Φ, which could mean either being answerable for Φ or being accountable for Φ. This is because Scanlonian blame is conceptualized as a response to perceived relationship impairment, whereby the notion of impairment is not specific enough. This becomes apparent if we compare the following two scenarios. In the first of these scenarios, "Anniversary,"

---

[14] The symbol Φ is used here to designate objects of moral appraisal in general.

a husband continues to offer his wife a bunch of carnations for their wedding anniversary year after year. In so doing, he ignores her "subtle but increasingly forceful hints" that she would prefer another sort of present and carnations are in fact her least favorite flowers (p. 620). In the second scenario, "Cheating," a husband has been having multiple affairs behind his wife's back. In each scenario, the relationship impairment, which grounds Scanlonian blame, is of two different kinds. In "Anniversary" the impairment is due to lack of good will, while in "Cheating" it is due to ill will. As a result, "Cheating" is simultaneously a case of answerability and accountability. By contrast, "Anniversary" is a case of answerability without accountability. This is because accountability involves a breach of a specific moral obligation. To be accountable for Φ, a person should be capable of grasping the reasons that make Φ morally impermissible. Yet, the inattentive husband doesn't breach a specific moral obligation: offering carnations to someone who doesn't care much for them can hardly be considered as morally impermissible. What's more, the inattentive husband does not seem able to grasp the reasons that speak against offering carnations to his wife: he fails to register her hints.

Finally, there are further scenarios, in which the three conceptions of responsibility come apart. To illustrate this, suffice to consider the following thought experiment: humans live side by side with some intelligent aliens who have a highly idiosyncratic moral code. For instance, they deem it morally impermissible to walk on the grass. A man who, naturally, fails to grasp the rationale for this prohibition walks on the grass believing that no aliens are present. If the aliens were to catch him in the act, they would be entitled to resent him: both his character and his reasons for the trespass would be open to their negative moral appraisal. That is to say, he would be rightly held responsible by the aliens in the sense of both attributability- and answerability-responsible. However, it would be inappropriate for them to also hold this man accountable for walking on the grass. On this third conception of responsibility, his actions should be exempt from responsibility.[15]

---

[15] In Shoemaker's view, a psychopath may be considered, by analogy, as attributability- and answerability-, but not accountability-responsible. See Shoemaker (2009) where this line of thought is further developed.

The important point made here is that the aliens do not have to choose between different conceptions of responsibility: assuming the validity of their moral code, the correct response to the man's trespass is to impute responsibility in terms of both attributability and answerability while granting exemption from responsibility in terms of accountability. This point is of great significance to the present inquiry since it appears to support the idea that volitional and non-volitional conceptions go wrong because they attempt to provide a comprehensive account of responsibility and to oust the alternative. This is consistent with some of the conclusions we reached so far: as shown throughout this and the preceding chapter, neither a volitional, nor a non-volitional conception suffices to offer a comprehensive account; at the same time, however, neither can be completely ignored. Shoemaker's proposal explains this upshot by suggesting that no comprehensive account of responsibility can also be unified. For responsibility is a cluster concept covering at least three niche conceptions which are irreducible to each other: attributability, answerability, and accountability.

This is a plausible explanation: looking at the preceding argument reconstruction, Wallace's volitional conception can be easily mapped onto responsibility as accountability while Smith's non-volitional conception bears closest resemblance to responsibility as attributability.[16] Moreover, the disagreement between the two conceptions can be cast as an attempt to integrate most cases of responsibility that in Shoemaker's terms would fall under answerability into the scope of accountability, if we take a volitional stance, or attributability, if we take a non-volitional one. Each conception would then proceed to reject the responsibility-type that does not fit in as either derivative, in the case of attributability, or superfluous, in the case of accountability.[17]

---

[16] In her response to Shoemaker, Smith (2012) argues that her rational relations view should not be associated with attributability but answerability which is the only responsibility in the strict sense. Having engaged closely with this argument in the previous section, I shall not comment on it any further.

[17] In the course of the earlier discussion, it has become clear that attributability is made vulnerable to a volitional objection of being a secondary kind of moral responsibility in virtue of its closer association with character assessment viz. aretaic appraisal rather than agency in the strict sense. However, in what sense could accountability be seen as superfluous given its direct link to moral obligation? By superfluous here I do not mean to suggest

Notwithstanding, there are two compelling reasons which speak against the overall framework of Shoemaker's proposal. The first is that the distinction between three irreducible responsibility conceptions rests on an unchecked assumption. This assumption is that the great variety of moral appraisal that may be legitimately bestowed onto Φ points to a disunity in the conditions, under which it is fair to hold an agent responsible for Φ. Yet, as the examples discussed by Shoemaker indicate, the differentiality of moral appraisal is explained just as easily, if not better, by inherent differences within Φ, the category of things that one could be plausibly held responsible for. Such differences are perfectly compatible with a unified conception of responsibility. For instance, the fact that moral appraisal should differ significantly when directed at different objects, including conflicting attitudes, regrettable inattentiveness, and a callous betrayal of trust, to use Shoemaker's own examples, is unsurprising, for it is self-explanatory. To make sense of it, we do not need to posit, as Shoemaker does, the validity of three separate conditions of responsibility applicable to each of these cases. That is to say, citing differentiality of moral appraisal is at best ineffectual here as the conclusions that Shoemaker draws about the disunity of responsibility as a concept do not follow from, but are only consistent with it; however, the opposite claim, unity of responsibility, is also consistent with differentiality of moral appraisal.

The second reason for rejecting the overall framework of Shoemaker's proposal is that the three conceptions of responsibility—attributability, answerability, and accountability—clearly aim to answer the same kind of questions and to address related concerns. More specifically, all three conceptions concur in answering two main questions: What makes Φ

---

that proponents of a non-volitional account, such as Smith's have to deny the relevance of accountability-type cases of responsibility, this would be an impossible, if not absurd task. Instead, accountability could be seen as superfluous a notion, some of its cases being recast as answerability-type situations and others as engaging primarily one's liability or legal as opposed to moral responsibility. I shall say more about the relationship between legal and moral responsibility in the subsequent section. In fact, Smith's response to Shoemaker (Smith 2012) follows precisely this dual tactic in rejecting responsibility as accountability: some aspects are absorbed into answerability and others presented as liability matters, such as punishment and compensation.

a legitimate object of moral appraisal? Under what conditions would it be fair to hold an agent responsible for Φ? In other words, they behave as conceptions specifying the workings of one and the same concept in different contexts rather than accounts of loosely related target concepts. As Shoemaker's analysis rightly points out, the responses given by these conceptions do not reach a level of generality to be expected from an overall theory of responsibility. This, however, can be explained by the fact that each of the conceptions stays too close to the phenomenon that provides its central case: conflicting attitudes, regrettable inattentiveness, callous betrayal of trust. And so, the insufficient generality of the answers provided does not warrant the conclusion that responsibility is merely a cluster concept. What it points to instead is the idea that neither of the three conceptions– attributability, answerability, and accountability—is successful in articulating the best way of conceptualizing responsibility. To the extent that there is a considerable overlap between these conceptions and the two competing volitional and non-volitional perspectives of immediate interest to the present inquiry, Shoemaker's discussion provides a useful diagnostic tool. For it enables us to see more clearly that no conception of responsibility that prioritizes one type of relevant phenomena at the expense of others, be it attitudes, patterns of awareness, actions, or violations of specific moral obligations, could provide a compelling overall theory of responsibility. Yet, we should be wary of making a further, unwarranted step which is to deduce from here that a compelling overall theory of responsibility could not be unified. In light of the convergence of underlying responsibility queries that we observed in the context of all three conceptions—attributability, answerability, and accountability—it seems promising to look for a more fundamental conception of responsibility which can successfully integrate insights from these local conceptions of responsibility as well as explain their apparent disagreements. To flesh out such a fundamental conception of responsibility will be a task undertaken at a later stage of the present inquiry. The remainder of this current chapter will aim to identify and explore the possible contribution that a non-volitional perspective, such as Smith's rational relations view, could make to understanding agency in the context of addiction.

2.4 **Addiction and agential evaluative stance**

Looking at the approaches to responsible irrationality available to us within the rational relations view, we find ourselves faced with a dilemma: either evaluative judgment is in fact a kind of voluntary control, not an alternative to it, or the non-volitional perspective targets some lesser kind of moral appraisal than the volitional one. However, having considered Shoemaker's critique of three alternative responsibility conceptions, we are in a position to identify a way out of this dilemma: by giving up its claim on comprehensiveness, the rational relations view could offer valuable insights into some aspects of responsible agency that a volitional view, such as Wallace's account of responsibility in terms of reflective self-control, is bound to miss out. This is particularly salient with respect to agency in the context of addiction, one of the focal points of the present inquiry. As we saw in Chapter 1, instances of addiction appear to be, at first blush, one of the paradigm cases that speak in favor of a volitional conception of responsibility. By concentrating on questions about how much and what kind of control over actions and choices is compatible with addiction, such a conception would track down responsiveness to reasons satisfactorily, assuming that reasons for action are somehow given in advance, "out there" awaiting the agent's recognition. There is a long-standing and fecund tradition behind this recognitional view of practical reason.[18] The following discussion won't be taking issue with it as a whole. The ambition instead will be to bring into relief some limitations of the picture of responsible agency in the context of addiction that flows from this recognitional view and to show how these limitations

---

[18] See Wedgwood (2003) for a discussion of the distinction between recognitional and constructivist conceptions of practical reason and reasons for action in particular. According to Wedgwood, recognitional views are often of Aristotelian descent and constructivist, of Kantian. As it will become clear from the argument in the subsequent chapters, I do not take Aristotle's philosophy to yield itself easily to either a recognitional or a constructivist interpretation and the Aristotelian account of responsible agency I propose aims to reconcile aspects of both approaches. For instance, an implication of this account is that valid reasons for action are neither only to be discovered (as the recognitional view claims), nor entirely construed by us (as the constructivist view claims); instead, they are partly discovered, and partly construed. I say more about this in Radoilska (2007, pp. 15–38; 191–210). See also Wiggins (1998) on the related dialectic of discovery and invention which seems to be implied by the notion of truth in ethics as a kind of practical truth.

might be rectified by adopting an alternative view centered round the agent's evaluative stance, such as Smith's rational relations view.

Drawing on the critical analysis of Wallace's account of addiction in Chapter 1, it becomes clear that on this volitional view addiction is relevant to responsible agency only in so far as it constitutes a sizeable obstacle to voluntary control. More specifically, if addiction undercuts both powers of reflective self-control identified by Wallace—the power to grasp and apply relevant, especially moral reasons, and the power to control or regulate one's behavior by the light of such reasons—it would provide a ground for comprehensive exemption. Alternatively, if addiction only affects the second power of reflective self-control, it would provide a ground for partial excuse or mitigation. As a result, addiction itself is never directly an object of moral appraisal. For it is not considered as a constitutive aspect of an addict's responsible agency but either an obstacle to it—when it grounds diminished responsibility—or a consequence of it—when the addict's powers of reflective self-control are still intact. As argued earlier, this marginalization of addiction proves unsatisfactory. Reactive attitudes, such as resentment toward people with addiction, do not appear to be wholly dependent on settling the question of whether they had sufficient powers of reflective self-control enabling them to recognize moral reasons and act upon them at a particular moment in time. Instead, these attitudes seem directed to the very constitution of agency in the context of addiction, not only to what's left to the addict's voluntary control. By redirecting the focus of moral appraisal to the evaluative stance of an agent with addiction as suggested by Smith's non-volitional conception, we would expect to be in a better position to account for addiction as an inherent, even constitutive aspect of an addict's responsible agency. But first, let us consider two pioneering portraits of addiction in modern European literature.

2.4.1 De Quincey: *Confessions of an English Opium-Eater*

In the concluding pages of this classic memoir of addiction, which was originally published in 1822, we read (2002, pp. 180–181):

> The interest of the judicious reader will not attach itself chiefly to the subject of the fascinating spells, but to the fascinating power. Not the opium-eater, but the

opium, is the true hero of the tale; and the legitimate interest on which the interest resolves. The object was to display the marvellous agency of opium, whether for pleasure or pain: if that is done, the action of the piece has closed.

Yet, the subsequent paragraphs tell the story of a full recovery from addiction, which the Opium-Eater manages without "benefit from any medicine," "after a seventeen years' use and an eight years' abuse" (p. 183). The explanation given for the success of this recovery is of particular interest for the purposes of the current analysis (pp. 181–182):

> The reader is aware that opium has long ceased to found its empire on spells of pleasure; it was solely by the tortures connected with the attempt to abjure it, that it kept its hold. Yet, as other tortures, no less it may be thought, attended the non-abjuration of such a tyrant, a choice only of evils was left; and *that* might as well have been adopted, which, however terrific in itself, held out a prospect of final restoration to happiness. This appears true; but good logic gave the author no strength to act upon it. However, a crisis arrived for the author's life, and a crisis for other objects still dearer to him—and which will always be far dearer to him than his life, even now that it is again a happy one. I saw that I must die if I continued the opium: I determined, therefore, if that should be required, to die in throwing it off.

To put this account into context, we should link it with an earlier observation about the kind of pleasure that opium can provide (pp. 93–94):

> . . . opium, I confirm peremptorily, is incapable of producing any state of body at all resembling that which is produced by alcohol: and not in *degree* only incapable, but even in *kind*: it is not merely in the quantity of its effects merely but in the quality, that it differs altogether. The pleasure given by wine is always mounting, and tending to a crisis, after which it declines: that from opium, when once generated, is stationary for eight or ten hours: the first, to borrow a technical distinction from medicine, is a case of acute—the second, of chronic pleasure: the one is a flame, the other is a steady and equable glow. But the main distinction lies in this, that whereas wine disorders the mental faculties, opium, on the contrary (if taken in a proper manner), introduces amongst them the most exquisite order, legislation, and harmony. Wine robs a man of his self-possession: opium greatly invigorates it.

The contrast with alcohol which frames De Quincey's discussion on the perceived benefits of opium clearly refers to a well-known distinction in classical philosophy, between the lower pleasures of the senses and the higher pleasures of the intellect and, to a lesser degree, moral sentiments. The former pleasures are standardly described as unstable, unsustainable, and ultimately corrupting; by contrast, the latter are defined as peaceful, lasting, and invigorating. A central exposition of the classical doctrine of higher vs. lower pleasures can be found in Aristotle's *Nicomachean Ethics*, Book VII, immediately after the discussion of weakness of will.[19] The analogy with the classical tradition becomes even more apparent in the following excerpt where the contrast with alcohol culminates in a striking apology of opium (pp. 95–96):

> I short, to sum up all in one word, a man who is inebriated, or tending to inebria-tion, is, and feels that he is, in a condition which calls up into supremacy the merely human, too often the brutal, part of his nature: but the opium-eater (I speak of him who is not suffering from any disease, or other remote effects of opium,) feels that the diviner part of his nature is paramount; that is, the moral affections are in a state of cloudless serenity; and over all is the great light of the majestic intellect.

This apology of opium is delivered in terms directly reminiscent of Aristotle's psychology, especially *On the Soul*, Book III and *Nicomachean Ethics*, Book X. Two elements of De Quincey's account deserve special attention. The first is the division of the human psyche into a purely human and even animal-like part, to the extent that some sensual expe-riences are shared with other non-human animals, on the one hand, and on the other, a divine or intellectual part. The second element is the implied link between opium as a higher pleasure of the intellect and gen-uine happiness, or eudaemonia, which Aristotle opposes to the ephem-eral and ultimately disappointing lower pleasures.[20]

Yet, there is an important disanalogy between the pleasures of opium as presented in De Quincey (2002) and the pleasures of the intellect on Aristotle's account. For instance, according to Aristotle, the pleasures of intellect are immune to the dangers of excess: this is, in fact, one of the central reasons for identifying them as higher pleasures, that is, pleasures constitutive of eudaemonia. In contrast, lower pleasures are deemed to be potentially distracting from, if not inherently hostile to, eudaemonia

---

[19] See also Chapter 4, Section 4.2 which expands on the link that Aristotle draws between akrasia and lower pleasures of the kind De Quincey associates here with alcohol, but not opium.

[20] There is no agreed equivalent of "eudaemonia" in the current philosophical parlance. Its most frequent counterparts include: "human flourishing," "the good life," and "happiness." To avoid confusion, I shall only employ the original term throughout the discussion.

in virtue of being prone to excess. Since De Quincey's apology of opium is punctuated by persistent caveats that the benefits of this "dread agent of unimaginable pleasure and pain" (p. 87) can only be had subject to disciplined and appropriate use, the pleasures of opium should be relegated to the category of lower pleasures of the senses.

The case for reclassification is further strengthened by the very fact that opium could also be the cause of pain, just as much as pleasure. For the superiority of intellectual pursuits as source of higher pleasures on Aristotle's account partly derives from the absence of pain that these pursuits could be legitimately associated with.[21] What's more, higher pleasures directly supervene upon the active exercise of one's own abilities.[22] They are not experienced primarily in virtue of some external object or occurrence, which is the case with lower pleasures. This is because receptivity defines the workings of the senses, in response to stimuli from outside. For instance, the pleasures of taste hinge on the availability of appropriate food or drink. In short, on this Aristotelian picture, higher pleasures are intimately related with activity and lower pleasures with passivity. An important corollary is that higher pleasures are by definition controlled and immune to the excesses that threaten to turn lower pleasures, such as eating or drinking, into their opposites—displeasures and even pains. By being in control of the activities, upon which higher pleasures supervene, an agent is also in control of these pleasures. Unlike lower pleasures, they cannot become overwhelming.

Once we take into consideration these points, a complete disanalogy between opium and the pleasures of the intellect becomes difficult to resist. Its openness to excess leading to nightmarish hallucinations and

---

[21] I have developed this line of argument in more detail in Radoilska (2007, pp. 255–272). For another state-of-the-art exposition of Aristotle's views on pleasure and pain and their ethical significance, see Frede (2006).

[22] Supervenience is a central notion in analytic philosophy. It denotes a relationship of dependence between different categories of properties or predicates. For instance, mental properties are said to supervene upon physical ones, evaluative, upon non-evaluative predicates. See, in particular, Kim (1993) and Jackson (1998), two seminal works on supervenience and its applications across different domains. Aristotle's discussion of the relationship between pleasure and activity is considered as the first instance where dependence is conceptualized in terms of supervenience.

almost total inactivity,[23] the very fact that it is indeed an object that gives pleasure in virtue of being physically consumed rather than, as it were, providing food for thought, clearly align opium with paradigm cases of lower pleasures and their stimuli, such as alcohol.

At this point, it might be objected that the inconsistency in De Quincey's treatment of the pleasures of opium that I was at pains to identify and explore is immaterial. Why should we care about it, since the *Confessions* are not a philosophical treatise, but a work of fiction? Does it really matter whether De Quincey got muddled about the classical distinction between higher and lower pleasures and misclassified opium as a result?

In response to this objection, there are two points to make. First, although the *Confessions* are a literary not theoretical opus, their author is taking due care in making his case about opium. For the memoir is still meant to provide us with an authoritative testimony, if not theory, of opium. Consider the following statement: "This is the doctrine of the true church on the subject of opium: of which church I acknowledge myself to be the only member—the alpha and omega" (De Quincey 2002, p. 97). The subsequent pages proceed to justify this claim of ultimate authority on the subject of opium. To this end, De Quincey points not only to his "large and profound personal experience" (2002, p. 97) but also to his familiarity with the scientific literature on the effects of opium available in his day. Second, in light of the author's excellent classical education, which is amply evidenced on the very pages of the *Confessions*, it is extremely unlikely that opium gets amid the higher

---

[23] The later parts of the *Confessions* abound with vivid recollections of both. Here is an example: "I could sooner live with lunatics, or brute animals. . . the unimaginable horror with which these dreams of Oriental imagery and, and mythological tortures impressed on me. . . I was stared at, hooted at, grinned at, chattered at, by monkeys, by paroquets, by cockatoos. I ran into pagodas: and was fixed for centuries, at the summit, or in secret rooms. I was the idol; I was the priest; I was worshipped; I was sacrificed. I fled from the wrath of Brama through all the forest of Asia: Vishnu hates me: Seeva laid wait for me. I suddenly came upon Isis and Osiris: I had done a deed, they said, which the ibis and the crocodile trembled at. I was buried, for a thousand years, in stone coffins, with mummies and sphinxes, in narrow chambers at the heart of eternal pyramids. I was kissed with cancerous kisses, by crocodiles; and laid, confounded with all unutterable slummy things, amongst reeds and Nilotic mud" (De Quincey 2002, pp. 169–171).

pleasures by mistake. Moreover, the level of detail and careful elabora-
tion in the relevant passages suggest that the association between opium
and the pursuits linked to superior pleasures is a deliberate strategy: it
brings to life the evaluative judgments that motivate the Opium-Eater
as an agent, and at the same time confers the idea that the rationale for
these judgments is based on an implicit confusion. Before expanding on
these remarks, let us first look in the next section at another memorable
portrait of addiction from nineteenth-century European literature.

2.4.2 **Dostoevsky: *The Gambler***

Unlike De Quincey's memoir, Dostoevsky's novel—also loosely based
on the author's own experience of what we would call today "problem
gambling"—ends with the lead character's, Alexey Ivanovich, utter
absorption in addiction instead of recovery. This finale is all the more
striking since, at the surface of it, Alexey Ivanovich starts gambling as
a way to obtain a large sum of money that could not be obtained in any
other legal, if not respectable, way in time to save from ruin the woman
he loves, Polina Alexandrovna. Yet, there are signs that gambling is not
just an unsavory means that he undertakes under duress, as it were.
For instance, reflecting on an episode from this initial stage when his
approach to gambling was outwardly instrumental, Alexey Ivanovich
makes the observation (2008, pp. 243–244):

> I do not remember whether I even once thought about Polina during all this. At
> the time I experienced some sort of irresistible pleasure in snatching and raking
> the banknotes, which were piling up in front of me. . . I distinctly remember that
> without even the slightest prompting of vanity, a frightful craving for risk suddenly
> took hold of me. It may be that by going through so many sensations the soul does
> not feel satisfaction but is only exasperated by them, and demands yet more sensa-
> tions, and stronger and stronger ones, until it is finally exhausted.

Two years on, when gambling has already become his primary occupa-
tion, Alexey Ivanovich meets with Mr. Astley, a former acquaintance,
whom Dostoevsky depicts as an impassive, though not unsympathetic
observer. The encounter, recorded from the Gambler's perspective proceeds as follows (pp. 269–270):

> He began to quiz me. I knew nothing; I hardly ever looked at the newspapers and
> had definitely not opened a single book since I had been there.

"You've become dull," he commented; "you have not only renounced life, your own interests and those of society, your duty as a citizen and a man, your own friends (and you did have friends)—you've not only renounced every aim what-soever in your life except for winning at gambling, you've even renounced your memories. I remember you at a passionate and intense period of your life; but I am sure that you have forgotten all your best impressions of that time; your dreams, the most urgent of your present desires, do not go beyond even and odd, rouge, noir, the twelve middle numbers, and so one and so forth, I'm sure of it!"

In fact, the Gambler himself seems to take a similarly dim view of his situation (pp. 265–266):

I have simply destroyed myself! But there is almost nothing to draw a compari-son with and it is useless to moralise on oneself! Nothing could be more absurd than moralising at a time like this. Oh, self-satisfied people: with what proud self-assurance these chatterboxes are prepared to deliver their maxims! If only they knew to what extent I myself understand how completely loathsome my present situation is, then of course they would not lash out at me, in the hope of teaching me. But what, what can they tell me that is new, that I do not know? And is that really the point? Here the point is that. One turn of the wheel and—everything changes, and these same moralists would be the first (I am sure of this) to come and congratulate me with friendly zest. And they would not all turn away from me as they do now. Yes, to hell with them, with all of them! What am I now? Zéro. What can I be tomorrow? Tomorrow I may rise from the dead and start to live again!

However, the focus of this negative self-appraisal differs from that of the damning verdict delivered by the impassive observer in the charac-ter of Mr. Astley. For the Gambler's self-deprecating comments are not directed at gambling per se, but only at being unsuccessful at gambling. This becomes apparent considering that the Gambler takes immense pride in winning on roulette. What is more, he remembers such lucky occasions in great detail, down to every single bet, as though they would be important achievements of his (p. 267):

Oh! That evening when I took my seventy gulden to the gaming table was also quite remarkable. I started with ten gulden and once again with passe. . . counting what I had before there was now one thousand and seven hundred gulden—and this in less than five minutes! Yes, in such moments, one forgets all one's previous failures! You see, I had achieved this at the risk of more than my life, I had dared to take the risk—now I was once again among the ranks of men!

This idiosyncratic understanding of gambling as a possible outlet for successful agency rather than sheer luck ties in with the Gambler's ruminations about strength of character, which by the end of the novel he associates with persevering with gambling and resisting the temptation to quit (p. 275):

> The most important thing is strength of character. I need only recall what happened to me in this respect seven months ago in Roulettenburg, just before I finally lost everything. . . when you are alone in a foreign country, far from home and friends, and not knowing what you will eat that day, you bet you last gulden, your very, very last! I won and twenty minutes later I walked out of the casino, with a hundred and seventy gulden in my pocket. . . But what if I had lost heart, if I had not dared to make that decision?

I shall say more about the distinctive fallacy on which the Gambler's idea of success in gambling rests in the concluding chapter of this monograph when I have expounded on the theory of action as actualization that would enable us to identify what exactly goes wrong with Alexey Ivanovich's evaluative judgment. At the present, however, I shall concentrate on the couple of related features shared by both Dostoevsky's and De Quincey's insightful portraits of addiction.

Firstly, the Gambler and the Opium-Eater make a similar mistake about the structure and contours of their agency. Both confer the respective centers of it on to something that patently falls outside the domain of agential control: luck in the one case, opium in the other. And so, the resulting, addiction-centered agency is paradoxical by its very nature. For it is eccentric in a self-defeating way: agential control is surrendered in search of a greater, though impossible, control. As a result, a form of passivity or dependence is placed at the heart of an addict's activities. This paradoxical transformation becomes possible—this is the second feature the Gambler and the Opium-Eater have in common—because the mirage of greater control and more successful agency is consistent with a very real experience of an intense, unusual pleasure. Mistaking it for the precursor of eudaemonia in the case of the Opium-Eater, of an independent existence in the case of the Gambler, the agent gets quite literally hooked to the pursuit of this elusive pleasure. In both cases, this patent mistake gets absorbed into a set of articulate and well-connected evaluative judgments that seems too sophisticated to raise immediate suspicion. More importantly, even though a closer look could easily unearth the irrationality of placing one's hopes as an agent on to the alleged proprieties of opium or luck on the gambling table, each of the two characters is at pains to avoid taking such a look. In this respect, addiction-centered agency as depicted by De Quincey and Dostoevsky is more akin to self-deception or motivated irrationality broadly conceived (cf. Pears and Pugmire 1982; Davidson 2004) than addiction on the volitional account proposed by Wallace (1994) or Frankfurt (1971) that Wallace partly draws on. In particular, the surrender of agential control for the sake of an illusion of control that we observe in the stories of the Gambler and the Opium-Eater has very little to do with loss of reflective self-control: their predicament does not seem to affect either the power to grasp and apply relevant, especially moral reasons or the power to control or regulate one's behavior by the light of such reasons. On the contrary, both characters take moral considerations quite seriously and spend a lot of their time thinking deeply about what they should and should not do. Against the backdrop of these rich, reflective inner lives, the notion of settling the question of responsibility in the context of addiction along the schema of happy versus unhappy addiction, acquiescence to versus sincere though impotent revolt against an uncontrollable compulsion appears to be unpersuasive. What is more, since addiction-centered agency unmistakably manifests itself in actions for reasons—though arguably problematic and open to criticism—compulsion does not seem to merit the central role it is often given in account of responsibility in the context of addiction.

This role seems to be widely accepted not only in the philosophy of action (e.g., Frankfurt, 1971; Wallace 1994; and to some extent Watson 2004), but equally in psychiatry, neuroscience, and addiction studies. For instance, ICD-10 (World Health Organization 1992) asserts that a sense of compulsion is a central descriptive characteristic of the dependence syndrome. In a similar vein, a recent editorial in the international journal of *Addiction* singles out increasing compulsion as a key feature to understanding the phenomenon (Sellman 2009). In support of this claim, Sellman cites neuroscientific evidence indicating that addiction involves processes outside the addicted person's consciousness, i.e., cues are registered and acted upon by evolutionary primitive regions of the brain. He also refers to social studies on the low rates of long-term recovery from all kinds of addictions: less than 10% on average (Garner and Hardcastle 2004). Following this line of thought, it becomes plausible to interpret compulsion in terms of subjectivity irresistibility or diminished control.[24] We end up with the idea that addiction-centered agency, if it does not fall outside the domain of responsible agency altogether, would at best be insecurely perched on its margins. This upshot yields support to the dichotomy between the so-called disease and crime models of addiction in psychiatry and law, its philosophical counterpart being arguably a model of exemption from responsibility along the lines of Wallace's volitional conception. For all these otherwise divergent accounts of addiction share the same starting point: given that a specific moral or legal obligation has been violated by a person with addiction, does said violation engage this person's responsibility and, if so, to what extent?

I do not mean to suggest that this question is unimportant. However, having examined the two classical portraits of addiction offered by De Quincey and Dostoevsky, an exclusive focus on it seems unadvisable. By giving primary consideration to an addict's aptitude to conform to societal norms by exerting control over specific actions and choices, the question already implies the insignificance of his or her agential perspective. Once we side with Mr. Astley, we choose to ignore Alexey Ivanovich's reasons for gambling. In other words, once we assume that an impassive observer's account of putative norm violations suffices

---

[24] Two influential recent developments, which illustrate this line of thought, are the so-called incentive sensitization (Berridge and Robinson 2011) and ego-depletion (Levy 2011) theories of addiction. According to the first theory, addictive behavior, such as drug consumption, is pathologically motivated by uncontrollable urges in the presence of certain cues. Such cues or incentives are nearly irresistible because of the neurobiological changes underpinning incentive sensitization: once these changes take place, an addict would find it immensely difficult to act in light of reasons that speak against drug consumption whenever exposed to specific cues. According to the second theory, willpower is a limited resource that can be depleted. This is often the case with addicts who have to resist the urge to consume drugs, in addition to everyday tasks that also require the exercise of willpower. An implication of this theory is that if addicts breach an obligation in a state of ego-depletion, e.g., by breaking in to pharmacies to obtain the drug they crave, they should be exempt from responsibility.

for the purposes of settling the issue of an addict's responsibility, we have already adopted the view that addiction is compatible only with derivative moral agency, if any. As a result, the focus of moral appraisal unavoidably shifts toward issues, such as punishment and incentives for treatment, if not compulsory treatment for addiction, which indicate the tacit adoption of what Strawson (1962) dubbed objective as opposed to reactive attitudes toward agents with addiction.[25] The frequent use of moral, if not moralizing language in discussions of addiction does not provide a counterexample to this conclusion. As earlier reductive accounts of moral appraisal such as Smart (1961) have shown, the vocabulary of praise and blame can be employed superficially, to create incentives and disincentives, without implying any deeper evaluative or participatory commitment than the activity of grading apples. Recasting the discussion of responsibility in terms of evaluative judgment instead of reflective self-control offers the conceptual resources to avoid the implicit reduction of moral appraisal to liability management in the context of addiction. Yet, to take advantage of these resources, it seems that we should give up one of the central tenets of Smith's rational relations view, the emphasis on rational judgment. As shown by the preceding analysis, this emphasis leads to an unduly restrictive and ultimately conflicting account of what makes an agent's evaluative stance a better ground for moral appraisal than control over actions and choices. In this respect, an alternative non-volitional account that pays attention to the agent's motivational set in its entirety, that is, to the whole self, not just conscious reasons for action, seems to be more promising. To find out whether this promise could be kept, an exemplar of such an account, Nomy Arpaly's quality-of-will conception of responsible agency, will be critically explored in Chapter 3.

---

[25] See, for instance, Strawson (1962, p. 9): "If your attitude towards someone is wholly objective, then though you might fight him, you cannot quarrel with him, and though you may talk to him, even negotiate with him, you cannot reason with him. Seeing someone, then, as warped or deranged or compulsive in behaviour or peculiarly unfortunate in his formative circumstances—seeing someone so tends, at least to some extent, to set him apart from normal participant reactive attitudes. . . We look with an objective eye on the compulsive behaviour of the neurotic or the tiresome behaviour of a very young child, thinking in terms of treatment or training."

Chapter 3

Weakness of will and moral appraisal

Could responsibility be consistently conceptualized without a notion of control? In this chapter, I shall look into another kind of non-volitional conception which could underpin an affirmative answer, Nomy Arpaly's quality-of-will-based account. This account is particularly relevant to the present inquiry because it aims to ground a comprehensive theory of responsibility by reflecting on a special case of akrasia, the so-called inverse akrasia, whereby the akratic action apparently warrants positive moral appraisal in the absence of agential control.[1] The discussion will proceed as follows. I first reconstruct the central claim of Arpaly's quality-of-will-based account—agential control is irrelevant to the moral appraisal of actions—and expand on its implications (Section 3.1). I then explore instances of standard akrasia and show that they are consistently at odds with the idea of a responsible, yet uncontrolled action endorsed by the quality-of- will-based account (Section 3.2). Next, I consider in some detail three putative instances of inverse akrasia and conclude that the underlying notion of praiseworthy action in the absence of agential control rests on a mistake, which is to merge an agent's practical and theoretical perspectives over what constitutes a good reason for action (Section 3.3). Finally, I point to a residual challenge that flows from the quality-of-will perspective, which is to clarify the relationship between strength and goodness of will (Section 3.4). If this relationship turns out to be contingent, then at least the first of the two background assumptions of the present inquiry, according to which

---

[1] As in the previous two chapters, I shall continue to use "weakness of will" and "akrasia," viz. "weak-willed" and "akratic" interchangeably. The usefulness of a strict distinction between the two terms will be the topic of Chapter 4.

the issue of how to conceptualize responsibility is fundamentally about the nature and scope of moral appraisal, will turn out to be problematic.[2]

3.1 **Arpaly on responsibility in the absence of control**

In *Unprincipled Virtue* (2003), Nomy Arpaly argues that reflective self-control is not necessary for moral responsibility; what matters instead is a person's response to moral reasons as expressed in her actions independently of whether she is aware of these reasons or not.[3] Arpaly considers actual responsiveness to reasons to be a better indicator of the moral worth of agents than what is revealed in their practical deliberation or retrospective first-personal accounts. For such articulate self-conceptions are incomplete and often mistaken. What is more, they present the judgments an agent endorses on reflection as particularly authoritative at the expense of considerations that she either does not recognize or wishes to disavow, but are nevertheless part of her motivational set.[4] Yet, according to Arpaly, all elements of the latter are equally important with respect to an agent's moral and wider rational appraisal; for they all—jointly—manifest the quality of her will. Arpaly (2003, p.61) summarizes the conception of rationality which underlies her view of responsiveness to reasons in general and moral reasons in particular in the following list of four provisions:

> (1) A theory of rationality should not assume that there is something special about an agent's best judgement. An agent's best judgement is just another belief, and for something to conflict with one's best judgment is nothing more dramatic than ordinary inconsistency of belief, or between beliefs and desires. (2) When discussing beliefs, one should count all the beliefs the agent actually has, not only the beliefs that she has at the time of deliberation. . . (3) . . . For one to have a

---

[2] The second assumption—that there is a robust, yet defeasible link between being responsible and being (rightly) held responsible—does not seem to be immediately affected. I shall return to this issue in Chapter 4, where I focus on the residual challenge.

[3] For an illuminating overview of the main argument by Arpaly herself, see chapter 1 of her second monograph *Merit, Meaning, and Human Bondage* (2006).

[4] On the notion of motivational set see the seminal paper "Internal and External Reasons" by Bernard Williams. The distinction between internal and external reasons, drawn in this paper, informs the literature on inverse akrasia. More specifically, Williams argues that only internal reasons, i.e., reasons present within a person's motivational set—whether explicitly or inexplicitly—could constitute this person's reasons for action.

reason, one does not need to believe, or be disposed to believe that one has a reason. Finally (4) for an agent to be acting for a (good) reason R, she does not need to know that she is acting for (good) reason R.

According to Arpaly, this conception of wider rationality is not unduly revisionist, but in fact makes better sense of our ordinary practices of allocating moral praise and blame than accounts focused on deliberation and explicit views. To support this claim, Arpaly draws attention to a cluster of cases where praise is given to "good people with bad principles" who manage to do the right thing without being able to recognize that this is so. In such cases, we do not dismiss their good actions as lucky accidents with little relevance to the appraisal of these people as moral agents. Instead, we are inclined to write off the misguided principles upon which they ultimately do not act, or as Arpaly (2003, p. 9) puts it: "we do not say, 'He's a bad person, but luckily he's weak-willed.' We say, 'He's a good person. Unfortunately, he has those silly views, but you can safely ignore them.'" This is because, Arpaly points out, some good people "happen to be very bad at abstract thinking," and so, doing the right thing against their confessed principles might not lead to them revising these principles. In this respect, the cases at issue fit with the now standard conception of akrasia as acting against one's better judgment.[5] The parallel has already been drawn in an earlier paper, in which Arpaly and Schroeder (1999, pp. 161–162) introduce the term "inverse akrasia" to refer to these cases:

> The most commonly discussed examples of akrasia centre around wrongdoing of one sort or another, in which desires override judgement: one is on a diet, but somehow cannot help but eat the slice of cake; one is resolved to tell an awkward truth, but somehow a lie slips out. In the cases of interest to us, however, akrasia results in what, for lack of a better word, might be called rightdoing of one sort or another. That is, the akratic course of action is superior to the course of action

---

[5] This conception has been first defended in "How Is Weakness of the Will Possible?" (2001) by Donald Davidson. Originally published in 1970, this seminal paper argues for the possibility of weakness of will, which it explains as an action against an agent's all-things-considered rather than unconditional or sans phrase evaluative judgment. See also Mele (1987), which develops further the Davidsonian conception of weakness of will and offers and account of strict akratic actions as free, intentional, and uncompelled, yet performed against an agent's better judgment at the time of action.

recommended by the agent's best judgment. Because these cases reverse our usual expectations from akratic action, we call them cases of inverse akrasia.

Mark Twain's character Huckleberry Finn provides one of the central vignettes for inverse akrasia: having being brought up within a slave-owning class, he considers himself under the obligation to turn in Jim, a runaway slave. Yet, whenever the opportunity arises, Huck finds himself unable to do so. Still, this does not make him question the morality of his class and upbringing. Instead, he resigns himself to being a "bad boy" incapable of living up to his obligations.

Arpaly (2003, p. 9) points out that from an Aristotelian, as well as Kantian, perspective Huck's actions would not be acknowledged as morally significant, but only as a welcome expression of natural virtue—in the former case—or an inclination that happens to pull in the same direction as duty—in the latter case.[6] She considers this upshot to clearly put both these perspectives at a theoretical disadvantage and to expose the mistake, upon which they apparently rest, that to unduly tie up moral worth to a notion of reflective self-control; conversely, by implementing the four rationality provisions listed earlier, a quality-of-will-based account of praise- and blameworthiness has the advantage to capture the moral worth of inverse akrasia. In doing so, it enables moral theory to catch up with the more holistic practice of ordinary moral appraisal.

Arpaly (2006, p. 15) sums up this account as follows: "A person is praiseworthy for taking a morally right course of action out of good will and blameworthy for taking a morally wrong course of action out of lack of good will or out of ill will." "Good will" here indicates respon-siveness to pertinent moral reasons, "ill will"—the motivation to per-form an action for the very reasons that make it morally wrong, and "lack of good will" cover various failures to respond to pertinent moral reasons, also referred to as instances of "moral indifference." Given the holistic interpretation of responsiveness to reasons adopted by Arpaly, it becomes possible to see Huck's self-proclaimed failures to turn Jim in as

---

[6] On Kant's notion of actions in conformity with duty, but not from duty, see Chapter 1, Section 1.5. I shall say more on Aristotle's account of would-be inverse akrasia in the fol-lowing discussion (see Section 3.3).

morally right actions performed out of good will; for they are motivated by Huck's consideration for Jim as a fellow human being rather than, say, by defiance to established order or dislike of Jim's owner. Thus, far from detracting from the moral worth of his actions, the fact that Huck is able to respond to the pertinent moral reasons in spite of the appallingly misguided moral outlook his upbringing has provided him with seems to warrant even greater praise for Huck's inadvertent, or as Arpaly calls it—unprincipled, virtue.

Inverse or praiseworthy akrasia poses a significant challenge to theories that propose to conceptualize responsibility in terms of control: for it seems to display a clear-cut case where the responsibility and control come apart. Assuming that akrasia is indeed the exemplar of failing agential control it is often presented to be, and even if standard or blameworthy akrasia may leave us undecided as to the target of appropriate blame by lumping together two plausible candidates, failing agential control and a reprehensible action, inverse or praiseworthy akrasia seems to clearly single out the target of appropriate praise, a commendable action in the absence of agential control.

Thus, a quality-of-will-based account has two apparent advantages. Firstly, by focusing on the quality of will an agent expresses in her actions, it clearly recognizes attitudes as objects of moral appraisal in their own right. Secondly, a quality-of-will-based account treats positive on a par with negative moral appraisal. Yet, these advantages seem to be tied in with a less compelling idea: the insignificance of the first-personal or agential perspective for the purposes of moral appraisal. As we shall see throughout the subsequent analysis, this idea seems inescapable if we are to make sense of responsibility in spite of agential control.

3.2 **Standard akrasia**

The claim I shall critically examine in this section—agential control is irrelevant to the moral appraisal of akratic actions—can be broken down into the following components:

(1) Positive responsibility amounts to responsiveness to pertinent (moral) reasons or acting out of good will;

(2) In contrast, agential control is about implementing, or acting in accordance with one's better judgment; and

(3) One's better judgment is simply the judgment that an agent—rightly or wrongly—takes to be her better judgment as to what she should do; hence,

(4) Agential control does not presuppose responsiveness to pertinent (moral) reasons, but is consistent with defiance or indifference to such reasons, that is, with ill will or lack of good will. Hence,

(5) Akrasia only warrants blame when acting against one's better judgment adds up to a reprehensible action, a kind of wrongdoing; when it adds up to a commendable action, a kind of rightdoing—praise is due. Therefore,

(6) Agential control is irrelevant to the moral appraisal of akratic actions.

The thrust of the forthcoming argument will be to show, against (4), that agential control does presuppose responsiveness to pertinent reasons and that this insight is lost because premise (3) does not do justice to what makes the judgment, an akratic agent acts against better than the one she follows. To this end, I shall look more closely at standard instances of akrasia. As we shall see, the picture that emerges on inspection is more complex than the commonplace description "acting against one's better judgment" would allow us to gather. In fact, once reconstructed in full, this picture rebuts any notion of responsibility in spite of agential control, for akratic wrongdoings are responsible actions only in so far as they are demonstrably up to the agent in a sense that requires relevant agential control.

Before engaging in the argument proper, however, let me first make a point of clarification about the breakdown of the claim at issue, I offered earlier: I put in brackets "moral" to indicate that this claim implies a strict distinction between moral and non-moral reasons for action, which seems at odds with the otherwise holistic approach to reasons championed by the quality-of-will-based account of responsibility. Although I do not believe that such a stark distinction in the realm of practical considerations is either feasible or even desirable, I do not think that it is necessarily incongruous with the kind of holism Arpaly adopts, for its main purpose is to reinforce the moral insignificance of first-personal as distinct from third-personal considerations. So this is not a line of inquiry I shall pursue further at this stage.

Returning to the task at hand, let us start by considering the examples of standard akrasia Arpaly and Schroeder give in their 1999 paper (p. 161): "one is on a diet, but somehow cannot help but eat the slice of cake; one is resolved to tell an awkward truth, but somehow a lie slips out."

Both examples seem to point to the following picture:

> P$_1$: An akratic action A takes place when an agent fails to refrain from A whilst believing that she ought to refrain from A, or a type of actions to which A unmistakably belongs.

On this picture, whether an action is weak-willed or not hangs on settling a single question:[7] whether the agent refrains from performing A, or doesn't. The impression is reinforced by a terminological adjustment in defining akrasia as acting against one's *best* (instead of the conventional "better") judgment that we find time and again in both the paper quoted earlier and later work by Arpaly (e.g., 2003, 2006): the superlative "best" singles out a particular judgment as the only reference point that matters, whereas the comparative "better" indicates that there are two separate, opposing judgments, and that the one that takes precedence in defining the agent's course of action, though inferior in a significant way, is nevertheless able to catch her imagination. This is consistent with an alternative picture of akrasia, which is as follows:

> P$_2$: An akratic action A takes place when by performing it an agent fails to engage in B she correctly identifies both as worth undertaking simpliciter and worthier undertaking than A, which she also correctly identifies as a minor, trivial trespass, and in this sense, not worth undertaking simpliciter; nevertheless, she is drawn to A.

On this second picture, the failure that we should be interested in is that to engage in B rather than that to refrain from performing A, the latter

---

[7] On "settling a question" as an illuminating way of conceiving responsibility for both actions and attitudes, see Hieronymi (2008), which expands on the claim that "to intend to φ is to settle positively the question of whether to φ."

becoming an issue in so far as it unavoidably adds up to the former. What is more, akrasia emerges as a moral problem to the extent that it is also a problem of agential control: if a minor distraction of an A-type is able to throw an agent off her track and bring her good intentions to a halt, this could lead as easily to breaches of specific moral obligations the agent recognizes and intends to fulfill, e.g., telling the truth even though this might be awkward as to failures to accomplish innocent self-regarding objectives, e.g., getting oneself back into shape—to revisit the pair of examples suggested by Arpaly and Schroeder.

In the remainder of this section, I shall aim to flesh out the account of akrasia roughly sketched in P_2. However, let me first outline two worries about P_1 which give us a prima facie reason to go beyond this neat and elegant picture toward something more complicated, such as P_2.[8] The first worry is that P_1 doesn't seem to give us enough to effectively settle the question of akrasia that it invites us to contemplate: whether the agent refrains from performing A as she believes she ought to, or doesn't. This is because, by looking at P_1, we cannot tell whether it was up to the agent to refrain from A; and so, akrasia may not be correctly described as an action proper, say, eating a slice of cake, but merely as a failure to exercise self-control that results in a slice of cake getting eaten. In other words, P_1 leaves it an open question whether there is an akratic action for which to allocate responsibility, in addition to the failure to act in accordance with one's best judgment. The second worry is that, if we wish to rescue the notion of an action proper being performed against one's best judgment, we may have to abandon that of akrasia as a distinctive phenomenon, not just a sudden change of heart or a case of giving up on a tall order. For, if akrasia amounts to a person deciding, when the moment of action arrives, that what her best judgment demands from

---

[8] The difference between the two pictures of akrasia relates directly to that between the so-called single-judgment and two-judgment accounts of weakness of will. The latter take inspiration from Gary Watson's now classic challenge to the notion of free action contrary to one's better judgment in "Scepticism about Weakness of Will" (1977) where Watson argues that since weakness of will involves inability to resist some temptations, akin to compulsion, it should be interpreted as a kind of unreasonable change of mind. Hence, the need to look at two separate judgments, not just focus on the better one as in the standard conception. See Mele (2012) for a recent defense of the former, single-judgment account.

her is just too difficult, eating the slice of cake would be indeed an action proper, something that an agent does intentionally. At the same time, however, akrasia would collapse into a mere failure to stick to one's plan, akin to Richard Holton's notion of weakness of will as unwarranted readiness to revise one's prior resolutions (2009)—on this occasion, getting oneself back into shape.[9] It would then be clearly appropriate to assign responsibility for akratic actions. Yet, they would no longer be able to serve the purpose they are meant to serve in the dialectic of a quality-of-will-based account: these actions would be responsible to the extent that they are up to the akratic agent who, at the last moment, changes her mind—rightly or wrongly—about the practicality of her best judgment. In other words, failing agential control would not be failing with respect to the akratic actions: they turn out to conform to the volitional picture of responsible action as up to or controlled by an agent that a quality-of-will-based account wishes to challenge.

For the sake of clarity, let us sum up the two worries about P_1 in the form of a dilemma. To recap, according to P_1, an akratic action A takes place when an agent fails to refrain from A whilst believing that she ought to refrain from A. This leaves us with the following open question: If, on the one hand, the agent fails to refrain from A, as her best judgment dictates, why should we treat A, the resulting failure, as an action at all? On the other hand, if A is an action proper, why think of it as involving any loss of agential control? In both cases, P_1 fails to support the assumption upon which the quality-of-will-based account heavily relies: agential control is irrelevant to the moral appraisal of akratic actions. In the first case, this is because the lack of agential control is such as to call into question the very notion of akratic *actions*. In the second case, this is because responsibility for akratic actions comes along with agential control, for such actions are performed in accordance with an agent's revised, though not best, judgment.

For polemical purposes, this upshot might be sufficient: the conception of akrasia meant to underpin a quality-of-will-based account does not

---

[9] See also MacIntyre (2008) for a more radical conception along the same lines, concluding that conflicts of desire that become apparent in standard akrasia are in fact paradigmatic of our human condition as agents.

deliver the much-needed instances of responsibility for action without agential control. Yet, the conception at issue arguably rests on an incomplete description of the phenomenon, and so the doubt remains that a finer-grained description of akrasia might be more successful. Hence the need to develop a more compelling conception of akrasia along the lines of the proposed P_2 and to revisit the links between responsibility and control in this context.

To recall, P_2 states: an akratic action A takes place when by performing it an agent fails to engage in B she correctly identifies both as worth undertaking simpliciter and worthier undertaking than A, which she also correctly identifies as a minor, trivial trespass, and in this sense, not worth undertaking simpliciter; nevertheless she is drawn to A. So, unlike P_1, which makes akrasia revolve around A, one specific action contravening the agent's best judgment, P_2 separates out two logically distinct aspects of akrasia: one, an akratic action A; and two, an akratic failure to exercise self-control. For, on P_2, akrasia consists in failing to do B by doing A rather than failing to refrain from doing A simply by doing A as suggested by P_1. So, responsibility for akrasia could go beyond responsibility for an akratic action. Prima facie at least, the concurrent failure to exercise self-control by straying from the better course of action B looks like a plausible candidate in its own right.

The failure of interest to us is not just a failure to perform B. The notion of secure competence[10] recently proposed by Joseph Raz (2011, pp. 245–246) could help clarify this point:

> The sphere of our secure competence demarcates the basic domain in which we are competent rational agents, capable not only of planning and intending, but of acting. It is the domain in which our capacities of rational agency are [reliably] available to us, where. . . we do not need to assess our chances of success before we take an action. . . Agency presupposes the availability of such actions.

By performing an akratic action A instead of going ahead with the better course of action B she is able to identify, an agent not merely narrows

---

[10] Although both have to do with outlining the contours of autonomous agency, the notion of secure competence is to be distinguished from that of mental competence viz. decisional capacity. On the latter notion, see Radoilska (2012b).

down the domain of her secure competence—B is effectively taken out of it. She does so as a consequence of having undermined her own chances to develop and sustain such a competence. And so, a two-dimensional structure emerges from the apparently simple notion of akrasia as a failure of agential control: on the one hand, there is failure to perform B, the better course of action; and on the other, there is insecure, if not absent, competence as an agent, the background condition needed for A, the akratic course of action to become an option.

The advantage of introducing not only a second course of action, but also a dispositional background into the sketch of akrasia might not be immediately apparent. It is therefore worth considering the following pair of reasons in support of this move. Firstly, unless we bring into the picture the akratic agent's insecure competence as relevant background, in addition to the akratic action itself, we have not effectively moved away from the sketch of akrasia in P_1. More specifically, P_2 would remain vulnerable to the second worry, according to which all that happens in akrasia is a change of mind as to the practicality of the better option. By putting the spotlight on the insecure agential competence which sets the scene for akrasia, we give ourselves the means to address this worry.

Secondly, by reconceptualizing akrasia as a failure to perform B because of insecure agential competence, we are able to address the first worry that has arisen with respect to P_1: Are we justified in considering A, the alleged akratic action, as an action at all? In light of P_2, A appears to be up to the agent. Voluntary control with respect to A is not only consistent with, it is also indicative of the akratic agent's insecure competence.

Thus, the seemingly complex P_2 ends up offering a straightforward account covering both the possibility of akrasia and its ethical significance. In standard instances of akrasia, the primary target of negative moral appraisal is not the akratic wrongdoing per se, e.g., eating a slice of cake, but the akratic disposition it hints at. The fact that the akratic pursuit is trivially wrong and perceived as such by the agent who succumbs to it is not trivial but vital to both correctly describing and assessing akrasia. In other words, from an akratic agent's perspective, the akratic action A she eventually performs is no match for the better course of action B she thereby foregoes—and by a long shot. If

A is clearly no match for B, the akratic agent would not see herself as jeopardizing, let alone betraying, her commitment to B by engaging in A: for A is by no means on a par with B in her esteem. We have here incommensurability of sorts:[11] getting a drink versus getting a successful career. The akratic agent is in no doubt about which the worthwhile course of action is, and which isn't. A appears to her so anodyne in comparison to B, as to sustain the misconception that her performing A can be no threat to her pursuing B.

The foregoing conceptualization takes lead from Aristotle's account of akrasia in *Nicomachean Ethics* 7. More specifically, it expands on the distinction between akrasia proper and akrasia broadly conceived. Whilst the former is confined to scenarios, in which some pleasures of the senses play the role of obviously inferior distractions, the latter involves pleasures that have a manifest social component, such as taking revenge on those who have wronged us. The reason for taking this second category of pleasures of less significant triggers for akrasia is the idea that they are less visceral than the pleasures afforded by food, sex, and drink. This does not mean that they are conceived of, by the same token, as less overwhelming. After all, anger at a perceived offence can be just as arresting as the urges of the flesh, and this is well acknowledged throughout the *Nicomachean Ethics*. Instead, the lures of akrasia broadly conceived are deemed secondary because they do not allow for as striking a contrast between the two options as in akrasia proper where the alternatives present different categories of pursuit, in Aristotle's terms, the good and the merely pleasant that the akratic agent correctly perceives as detracting from the good. This clear-cut difference in kind gets fuzzier in instances of akrasia in the broad sense, for the inferior alternative is not, as it were, out of the league as such. To return to the example of an akratic impulse to get back at someone who has wronged us, the main objection against indulging in it seems to be that of likely disproportionality, of going beyond redress and committing injustice

---

[11] Cf. Wiggins (1979): expanding on Aristotle's account, it is argued that weak-willed agents intentionally choose what they know to be a worse option when they could choose a better one; however, the values of these options are different in kind so that choosing the better would still lead to some uncompensated loss.

against this person, although our better judgment tells us not to. And yet, a less extreme reaction of the same kind is certainly called for: to search redress for injustices suffered is, in principle, a sound response to moral reasons. So the akratic course of action here may also be considered as appealing under the guise of the good, and not only that of the merely pleasant. In this respect, akrasia in the broad sense is more like being bad at weighing reasons for action against each other than underestimating the threat posed to one's responsiveness to reasons by trivial distractions, such as the pleasures of the senses.[12]

The fact that akratic actions are assessed as trivial by the akratic agent and engaged in because of their triviality appears to be a cornerstone of the psychology of akrasia all too easily overlooked. However, we need to be equally wary of the opposite danger, which is to lose sight of the gravity of akrasia by focusing on the triviality of its outward expression. As stated in the initial formulation of the account on offer P_2, an akratic action is, by the look of it, a trivial trespass: having a slice of cake or a drink that one shouldn't. We are now in a position to see why responsibility for akrasia neither begins nor ends with the akratic action: for in akrasia nothing significant happens at the level of actions, such as eating a cake or even deciding to eat a cake.[13] Instead, the centerpiece is the dispositional background that such actions hint at. As argued earlier, although the akratic agent correctly perceives the akratic option as no good, but merely pleasant, she fails to take due notice of the fact that the better option, which she correctly identifies as both worth pursuing in and of itself and definitely worthier than the akratic alternative, does not appeal to her as it should. In other words, what appears to her under the guise of the good is wrongly perceived as unpleasant. In the presence of akratic incentives, the response to good reasons she can manage is not only insecure, but partial at best.

---

[12] See Chapter 4, where I provide a more detailed reconstruction of Aristotle's account of akrasia. See also Tenenbaum (2007, esp. ch. 7) which draws a distinction between direct and oblique evaluative cognitions. In light of this distinction, akrasia becomes possible when an agent's better judgment is of the latter type and so can be overturn by the more vivid, albeit misleading appearance of the akratic course of action as valuable.

[13] On the notion of choices, decisions, and intentions as mental actions, see Chapter 1, Section 1.1.

In light of these observations, it becomes clear that akratic actions are not the focus of responsibility for akrasia. For they are not self-contained actions: their significance lies primarily, if not exclusively, in the fact that they echo a distinctive attitude or disposition, which makes them appear as anodyne, if not harmless pursuits in the first instance. This is not to say that akratic actions are not done freely and voluntarily. As argued earlier, the akratic agent exerts control with respect to both the conception and performance of akratic projects. And as we shall see in Chapter 4, it is not uncommon for such actions to be the result of careful planning and deliberation.[14] This upshot is at odds with a quality-of-will perspective: standard instances of akrasia emerge as poor responses to good reasons rather than good responses to reasons that have not being sanctioned by one's best judgment. For the latter is not a second-order response to one's responses to reasons, but a good first-order response which the akratic fails to give because of her insecure competence as an agent.

3.3 **Inverse akrasia**

The discussion of standard instances of akrasia offers two mains lessons. The first is that responsibility for akratic actions is grounded in a notion of agential control over these actions. And so, they can hardly provide a case of responsibility in spite of agential control. The second is that akratic actions are not that significant for the overall moral appraisal of akrasia. Blame, whenever appropriate, is targeted at the underlying akratic attitude or disposition, insecure agential competence. With these lessons in mind, let us now consider in some detail three putative cases of inverse akrasia: Inept Burglar, Neoptolemus, and Huckleberry Finn.

3.3.1 **Inept Burglar**

This first case expands on a vignette offered by Philippa Foot: "a burglar who was caught because he sat down to watch television in the house he

---

[14] See Wallace (2001) for an extensive discussion of well-planned akratic actions and the implications this set of phenomena has for understanding deliberation and practical rationality more broadly.

was burgling."[15] For the purposes of the present discussion, let us add to this description that the burglar was well aware of the unjustifiably high risk he was taking for the sake of a show, whose repeat he could have safely watched in a couple of days. Hence, he was acting against his better judgment or akratically, and this has resulted in a kind of right-doing, practically giving himself up. Does this mean that the inept burglar deserves praise for this? It certainly doesn't.

A proponent of the quality-of-will-based account might be eager to point out that this is no counterexample demonstrating inverse akrasia to be unworthy of praise: it was not meant to be one. Instead, the objective here is to eliminate the kind of akratic rightdoing that wouldn't do for a quality-of-will-based account and explain why not. This, in turn, will have a direct bearing on the possibility of praiseworthy akrasia.

The objection to make on behalf of a quality-of-will-based account is that Inept Burglar is not a case of inverse akrasia at all: by staying to watch television at the scene of the crime, the burglar displays no good will, just ineptitude to follow through his plan. In this respect, Inept Burglar falls within a subclass of standard akratic actions, whose underlying structure is as follows: an agent commits to a plan, but then fails to implement it for no good reason.[16] At first blush, when the plan is objectionable, as in Inept Burglar, this failure might seem praiseworthy; yet, on reflection, praise for this sort of akrasia is inappropriate, for the good that comes out of it is not something that the agent does, but an unintended consequence of his ineptitude. That we are dealing here with no more than an unintended consequence becomes apparent from the fact that considerations about the worthiness of the plan are entirely absent from the burglar's thinking. That is to say, by staying

---

[15] Cf. Foot (1995, p. 7): "There is no doubt but that there are different kinds of cases of contrary-to reasonness, and not surprisingly it is possible to contravene rationality in more than one way at the same time. I once read of a burglar who was caught because he sat down to watch television in the house he was burgling, thus adding the contrary-to-reasonness of imprudence to that of dishonesty. Because his actions were faulty in that he did not hurry away with the swag, we can say, if we like, that he *should* have done so."

[16] My analysis here draws on Alfred Mele's suggestion that the better judgment, against which an akratic acts, may sometimes be merely "executive" as opposed to evaluative (Mele 1995, p. 71).

behind, he does not respond, albeit inadvertently, to good moral reasons, as inverse akratic agents are meant to do, but merely fails to enact his indifference to such reasons. With respect to moral appraisal, Inept Burglar is a case of lack of good will, for which blame is due; the fact that the burglar has inadvertently sabotaged his own plan does not make him less culpable.

The moral of the vignette is that, in order to count as expressions of good will, akratic actions have to be genuine responses to the good moral reasons that speak in their favor, not unintended consequences of acting in an akratic way that happen to conform to these reasons. At the same time, however, the agent has to be unaware of his or her responding to good moral reasons. If this is not the case, inverse akrasia will no longer be akrasia in the sense required to show that responsibility could and should be assessed independently of agential control. And so, to play its part in the dialectic of a quality-of-will-based account, it looks as though inverse akratic actions have to be, on the one hand, intentional, that is, undertaken under the description that shows them to be morally praiseworthy, and on the other, unintentional under the same description, for the inverse akratic agent is, by definition, unaware of acting in a morally praiseworthy way when so acting as a matter of fact.

3.3.2 **Neoptolemus**

One of the characters in a Sophocles play, a decent young man, sets out to defraud a vulnerable person as the only means to ensure that a great and noble cause meets with success. Yet, as soon as he brings his plan to fruition, this character is so overwhelmed with shame and remorse that he undoes it all, while recognizing that this will most likely lead to the downfall of the important cause he is still fully committed to. According to Arpaly and Schroeder (1999, p. 162), this is "perhaps the earliest recorded" occurrence of inverse akrasia since Neoptolemus—the character of interest to us—"does the right thing, but does so against his best judgment." Interestingly, the case has also attracted Aristotle's attention who comments on it both at the start and at the end of his discussion of akrasia, which effectively warns against treating Neoptolemus as a case of akrasia.[17] For, as outlined earlier, on Aristotle's view, akratic actions are committed in spite of the agent's correct judgment that such actions should be avoided or, in the terms of the present discussion, have no good reasons to speak in their favor. Neoptolemus does no such thing: not only because he goes against a misguided judgment of his about what should be done, not a correct one, but also because he does so knowingly. Hence, Aristotle concludes, praise is due for Neoptolemus' action precisely because it is not akratic. In this context, a viable notion of praiseworthy akrasia is explicitly rejected. More specifically, it gets explained away as the upshot of a sophistry:

> For, because of akrasia, the person acts in the way contrary to that in which he supposes he should act; and because he supposes that good things are bad and that he should not do them, he will do good actions and not bad ones.[18]

On one reading, these observations rehearse the conclusions reached by looking into Inept Burglar. Yet, on another, they contain in a nutshell a demonstration of why praiseworthy akrasia is conceptually impossible, a demonstration that also tells us something important about the nature of moral appraisal. To make this point clear, it is essential that we pay close attention to the original Neoptolemus case, to which Aristotle refers, as it is presented in Sophocles' *Philoctetes*. The following discussion isn't meant as an illustration of the argument on offer, but as an integral part of it: for, as I aim to show, the initial appeal of praiseworthy akrasia owes a lot to reflecting upon cases that are less than fully fleshed out. To this aim, I shall first consider Neoptolemus' action and its significance as intimated by the plot of the play.

It is the tenth year of the war against Troy. A prophecy has revealed that the city can only be taken with the help of a miraculous bow, which Philoctetes has in his possession. The Greeks order Odysseus and Neoptolemus to go and retrieve the bow from the island of Lemnos, where Odysseus, at the behest of the army's commanders, abandoned a severely wounded Philoctetes ten years ago. Given the merciless treatment he received from his fellow countrymen, Philoctetes can hardly be expected

---

[17] *Nicomachean Ethics* 7.2 1146a18–22; 9. 1151b17–23.

[18] *Nicomachean Ethics* 1146a28–31.

to willingly assist them or even listen to their plea. Moreover, despite the horrible injury he suffered, he is still an excellent archer, with an invincible bow at hand. He could easily dispatch both Odysseus and Neoptolemus before they get the chance of closing in on him. In light of these considerations, the two honorable ways of acquiring the bow—persuasion and open contest—are very unlikely to prove successful. Odysseus points this out and suggests an alternative which, although unacceptable in ordinary circumstances, he believes should be employed in this particular case because of the high stakes involved. This alternative is to trick Philoctetes into handing over his bow. Odysseus argues that Neoptolemus is the one to do it, because he was too young to take part in the original expedition against Troy and Philoctetes has no reason to mistrust him. Furthermore, in acquiring the bow, Neoptolemus will be able to earn immortal glory, for, according to the prophecy, no one else but he could conquer Troy if armed with this invincible weapon. At first, Neoptolemus refuses to use deceit, as he considers this to be wrong without exception. Later on, however, he gives in because of Odysseus' senior rank and reputation for wisdom, as well as his own ambition. As predicted by Odysseus, Philoctetes falls for Neoptolemus' tale and entrusts him the bow. However, instead of bringing the trophy back to Odysseus, Neoptolemus feels ashamed of his actions, tells the truth, and returns the bow, even though he understands that this will make him a hated enemy to his fellow Greeks and deprive him of immortal glory.

Against this backdrop, it is clear that Neoptolemus telling the truth and facing the consequences is an expression of good will, for which he deserves praise. But is he unaware of the ethical significance of his action? And did he really believe that it was his duty to trick Philoctetes and leave him helpless on the island?

To answer the second question first, Neoptolemus announces his consent to Odysseus' plan as follows: "All right. I'll do it. I'll set aside my sense that it's wrong."[19] What's more, Odysseus has not tried to conceal the nature of his proposal, which he calls a crime.[20] Obviously then,

---

[19] Sophocles, *Philoctetes* 120.

[20] Sophocles, *Philoctetes* 79–85: "I know, boy, it doesn't come/naturally to you to be talking like this or to be planning/crimes. . . We can/demonstrate our honesty another time. Just for

Neoptolemus does not mistakenly consider himself under the obligation to cheat Philoctetes. He only surmises that he might be excused to do so. His supposition does not seem completely unreasonable, given the significance of the bow and Philoctetes' intransigence toward the Greek cause.[21] A further complication stems from the fact that the decision to cheat Philoctetes, right or wrong, does not seem to be for Neoptolemus to make: Odysseus, who is in charge of the mission, is happy to take all the blame for that.[22]

The first question, whether Neoptolemus is unaware that his (allegedly inverse akratic) action is the right thing to do, is just as easy to answer: for Sophocles makes him articulate the reasons in favor of recanting his earlier decision with enviable candor.[23]

To conclude, Neoptolemus shows praiseworthiness and first-personal control over the relevant action to be inseparable in a way that excludes the inadvertent expression of good will needed by a quality-of-will-based account. Whilst in Inept Burglar we saw a case of akrasia unworthy of praise, Neoptolemus offers us an action which is worthy of praise, yet by no means akratic.

3.3.3 Huckleberry Finn

If the foregoing argument is correct, this pair of cases should cancel out the prospects of praiseworthy akrasia. But what of Huckleberry Finn,

---

now, for/one little day, forget your principles and follow my lead./After that you can spend the rest of your life enjoying an/unmatched reputation for righteousness."

[21] Sophocles, *Philoctetes* 66–67; 1111–1268.

[22] Sophocles, *Philoctetes* 50–54; 121.

[23] Sophocles, *Philoctetes* 1224–1249: "Neoptolemus: I am going to undo a mistake I made earlier./Odysseus: Your words alarm me. What mistake is this?/N.: One I made in obedience to you and the whole/army. O.: What have you done that you shouldn't have?/N.: I used shameful deception and trickery in/catching him. . . I took his bow from him. I am going to/return. . . O.: Zeus! What are you about to say? You are not/thinking of giving it to him? N.: I was wrong to take it. I have no right to keep it/. . . O.: There is someone—someone who will stop you/from doing this. . . Every man in Greece—myself included!/N.: You may be wise, but your words are not./O.: Nor are yours—and nor will your actions be./N.: Perhaps not wise, but they are just—and that/matters more than wisdom. O.: And how is it 'just' to give something back that you/took under my direction? N.: I made a shameful mistake. I am going to try/to put it right."

the paradigm case reconstructed at the start of the chapter: Couldn't it open a midway path between Inept Burglar and Neoptolemus?

The pair of cases challenges the conception of rationality that underpins a quality-of-will-based account. More specifically, it is aimed at this conception's fourth proviso, according to which, in order to act for a good reason, an agent doesn't need to know that she is acting for this reason. This is hardly the case of Huckleberry Finn, who experiences his inability to turn Jim in as an unwelcome constraint, before resigning himself to being a bad boy. I agree that, by not turning Jim in, Huck acts out of good will, for which praise is due. However, his expression of good will is not inadvertent. It is reluctant. For, while treating Jim as a fellow human being and not somebody's property, Huck resents responding to the pertinent reasons, to which he responds. This, however, is not the kind of example that could revive the prospects of praiseworthy akrasia. To do so, the proponent of a quality-of-will-based account should present a case of a good though inadvertent, or first-order, response to pertinent reasons. In contrast, Huck's response is good though reluctant. But to respond reluctantly to a pertinent reason, one has to be aware of the pertinence of this reason. So, there are two logically distinct aspects of Huck's stance: a good first-order response to the pertinent reasons, and a second-order reaction to it. In this respect, there is a parallel to be drawn with Kant's vignette of an honest man who refuses to give false evidence in spite of mounting pressure.[24] As we saw in Chapter 1, this man's unhappiness with the consequences of acting morally does not detract from the worth of his actions.

Here is a possible objection. In Kant's vignette the agent's unhappiness has to do with the circumstance of the action, not the action itself. What if, as Huck's case seems to imply, the inability to turn Jim in is appreciated, from Huck's perspective, as a constraint, as something that he has no choice over at all. This sort of reluctance goes deeper than unhappiness with external circumstances. In fact, it looks more like a constitutional inability to commit a certain kind of wrongdoing regardless of whether one wrongly believes it to be one's duty. With respect

---

[24] *Critique of Practical Reason* 5:515–516.

to this constitutional inability, Huck seems closer to a different vignette proposed by Arpaly (2006, p. 136):

> [A] truth-seeker cannot tell the lie while at the same time... be who he is. Thus he can, at the same time, feel that not telling a lie would be the right thing to do and experience his inability to tell the lie as something resembling akrasia. Sure, it is the right thing to do, but why, for God's sake, is he the one who always has to do the right thing? This is the sort of situation in which a person, though being, both objectively and in her own experience, "her true self" can experience that very self as constraining, as forcing things on her.

Construed in this way, Huck's second-order reluctance would seem to demonstrate the insignificance of an agent's first-personal perspective for the purposes of moral appraisal. For, regardless of what Huck thinks about his praiseworthy actions, they still remain worthy of praise. If so, inverse akrasia is, after all, successful in showing that the moral appraisal of actions is independent from the agent's perspective on them; and similarly, responsibility for actions is independent from agential control. Like the truth-seeker from Arpaly's vignette, Huck neither approves of, nor identifies with, his praiseworthy actions. What is more, both characters seem constitutionally unable to refrain from doing the right thing.

To address this objection, let us consider the distinction between moral and psychological incapacity, introduced by Bernard Williams (1995). Whilst moral incapacity imposes a limitation on what an agent can attempt to do knowingly in virtue of her evaluative commitments, psychological incapacity is independent from such commitments. Thus, inability to bring oneself to betray the confidence of a friend is an example of moral incapacity, whereas a phobia of things one readily acknowledges not to be scary is an example of psychological incapacity.[25]

---

[25] The following excerpt from a memoir of depression offers a poignant illustration of the clash between evaluative judgment and emotional response by which Williams defines psychological incapacity: "I can remember lying frozen in bed, crying because I was too frightened to take a shower and at the same time knowing that showers are not scary. I ran through the individual steps in my mind: You sit up, turn and put your feet on the floor, stand, walk to the bathroom, open the bathroom door, go to the edge of the tub . . . I divided it into fourteen steps as onerous as the Stations of the Cross. I knew that for years I had taken a shower every day. Hoping that someone else could open the bathroom door, I would, with all the force of my body, sit up; turn and put my feet on the floor; and then feel so incapacitated and frightened that I would roll over and lie face down. I would cry again,

In order for the objection to work out, the constitutional inability experienced by Huck has to be psychological, not moral and at the same time—still to Huck's credit. If what we have in Huck's case, however, is moral incapacity, this would undermine the objection. For, although an agent may not be aware of her moral incapacity to perform an action in advance of considering this action, she gains insight into it, once she attempts to perform the action. What is more, moral incapacities—unlike psychological ones—can be eventually lost as a result of conscious effort, although not immediately or "at will": this can be achieved if the agent successfully disavows the evaluative commitments that prevent her from performing the action under consideration.[26] So, moral incapacities not only provide an agent with reasons for action that she is aware of; the salience of these reasons is also under her agential control. Consider the following:

> The agent cannot, of course, lose the incapacity at will: but that is not because it is peculiarly moral incapacity, but just because nothing one can lose at will is an incapacity. Moral incapacity is explained through the will, as I have tried to show, but it is not subject to the will. . . Of course an agent may come to see a moral incapacity of his as something with which he is no longer identified, and try to overcome it. But so soon as this is really his state of mind—as opposed to the familiar phenomenon of merely occurrent resentment at one's moral identity—then he has already lost the moral incapacity: not necessarily in the sense that he can now do the thing in question, but in the sense that if he cannot, it is no longer a moral incapacity, but rather one that is merely psychological.
>
> (Williams 1995, pp. 53–54)

In light of these observations, if what Huck and the truth-seeker exhibit is psychological rather than moral incapacity, their actions would no longer be subject to moral appraisal, positive or otherwise. Importantly, this is a conclusion we reach assuming a quality-of-will perspective. For

---

weeping because the fact that I could not do it seemed so idiotic to me" (Solomon 1998, pp. 48–49).

[26] On different interpretations of "at will," some of which are consistent with agential control, see Hieronymi (2009). As Hieronymi points out, the fact that we cannot make soup "at will"—cooking requires a series of intentional actions that take place over time—does not justify the conclusion that making soup is beyond our voluntary control. By contrast, the fact that we cannot believe "at will" suggests, according to Hieronymi, that the norms of belief do not allow for voluntary control on the part of believers.

these actions are not responsive to reasons in a way that would make them expressive of the agent's quality of will. Suffering from a phobia does not make one a coward. What it does is to make it impractical to express one's will with respect to things that trigger one's phobia. And so, moral appraisal does not apply to actions directly related to this or other psychological incapacities, although it certainly applies to the way one goes about such incapacities. The earlier conclusions about Huck's vignette stand therefore confirmed: his actions are praiseworthy not in spite, but in virtue of, his agential control.

Nevertheless, more needs to be said to fully address the objection. In particular, it may be unclear why, having distinguished two aspects in Huck's stance—a good first-order response to pertinent reasons and a second-order reaction to it—I take only the former, but not the latter to be relevant to Huck's moral appraisal. Would that not amount to agreeing with the spirit, if not the letter of Arpaly's account of inverse akrasia? For the thrust of this account is to show that the agent's first-personal perspective is irrelevant to moral appraisal.

The notion of an agent's first-personal perspective requires disambiguation.[27] For there are two separate things that it may cover. The first is an agent's practical consideration of what to do. It shapes the description, under which some actions are perceived as worth undertaking, intended, and performed.[28] This agential perspective is clearly not irrelevant to the moral appraisal of action. On the contrary, it is what makes such an appraisal appropriate. For instance, we distinguish between merely causal and moral responsibility by considering this perspective.[29] And so, it helps define the scope of moral appraisal. Similarly, when we consider some actions as expressive of a person's quality of will, we effectively reconstruct her reasons for action, the upshot of her practical consideration of what to do.

The second thing that the notion of an agent's first-personal perspective may cover is this agent's reflection on what has been done by her.

---

[27] The following discussion draws on Radoilska (2007, pp. 191–209).

[28] On the concept of description under which an action is intended, see Anscombe (1963).

[29] I say more on this distinction in Radoilska (2010).

The modality of this second kind of first-personal consideration is theoretical rather than practical. In this respect, we may even say that it is not first-personal in the strict sense. For the point of reflection is to revisit one's actions from an informed observer's perspective, to adopt a third-personal perspective toward oneself as an agent.[30] Although the upshots of a theoretical consideration may be integrated into further practical considerations, an agent's theoretical consideration is clearly irrelevant to the moral appraisal of her actions, upon which it is a reflection. For this kind of reflection does not form part of an agent's reasons for action. Instead, it is already an instance of moral appraisal, viz. moral self-appraisal which is possible in virtue of the agent's conscious detachment from her practical stance. So we can agree with Arpaly (2003, p. 9) that morally good agents sometimes happen to be very bad at abstract thinking and that this should not affect their positive moral appraisal. This, however, does not mean that we should acquiesce in the idea of inverse akrasia. For the poor reflection we should ignore for the purposes of moral appraisal does not belong to the agent's practical perspective, to her first-personal stance qua agent. To give an example, we might consider regrettable the fact that a remarkable musician is not very good at talking about his art. However, it would not occur to us to consider him any less brilliant as a musician because of this. Similarly, in cases of would-be inverse akrasia like Huck's, the poor judgment that we should discount for the purposes of moral appraisal is not, as Arpaly would have it, a bad principle held by a good person, but a poor reflection on a good principle acted upon by an agent who—as an agent—is to be judged on the principles that motivate her actions, not on the way she assesses these principles. In light of this distinction, it becomes clear that a person's professed moral principles may not be of particular relevance to this person's moral appraisal: in so far as these professed principles differ from the principles upon which she acts, they are—naturally—irrelevant to the moral appraisal of both actions and agent.

Thus, the appeal of inverse akrasia turns out to rest on a mistake, which is to merge an agent's practical and theoretical, viz. reflective

---

[30] This conception of reflection is consistently developed in Ricoeur (1990).

perspectives on her actions. Looking at volitional conceptions, such as Wallace's account of responsibility in terms of reflective self-control, this mistake seems easy to make.[31] For the main claim appears to be that unless reflection controls action, there is no legitimate object of moral appraisal. Yet, a responsible action is an action for a reason. It does not have to also be an action, the reason for which is correctly apprehended by the agent when engaged in an armchair reflection. If there is a mental conflict that cases like Huck's may illustrate, it would be between an agent's practical and theoretical perspectives on what constitutes a good reason for action. Importantly, this conflict would not affect the agent's competence as to make it insecure in a way similar to what we observed earlier in the context of akrasia. For the mental conflict encountered by morally good agents who happen to be bad abstract thinkers is not internal to their agential perspective. It does not unsettle the way they respond to reasons in action, although it hinders the reflective account they give of themselves as agents. In light of these considerations, we can see that, *pace* Arpaly, neither Aristotelian nor Kantian accounts of moral appraisal would have difficulty recognizing the moral goodness of bad abstract thinkers, such as Huck. For both Aristotle's and Kant's philosophies insist on a robust distinction between the practical and theoretical uses of reason.

3.4 Strength versus goodness of will

The case of morally good agents who are bad at abstract thinking is to be distinguished from cases where strength and goodness of will patently come apart. To appreciate this, let us consider a fine example of the latter category fleshed out by Yukio Mishima in his novel *The Temple of the Golden Pavilion* (2001).

3.4.1 Mizogushi

Mizogushi, a novice at a Buddhist temple, fights a sudden impulse to confess a crime whilst seeing off, in the midst of the congregation, the Temple's Superior. As Mizogushi correctly surmises, the Temple's

---

[31] This account is defended in Wallace (1994). For a critical discussion, see Chapter 1.

Superior has learned of this crime long time ago, but has decided not to bring it up in order to allow the novice to confess in his own time:

> It was at this point that a strange impulse was born in me. Just as when some important words were trying to break free from my mouth and were blocked by my stuttering, this impulse was held burning in my throat. The impulse was a sudden desire for release. At this moment, my previous ambitions—my desire to enter university, and still more the hope suggested by Mother that I might succeed to the Superior's post—ceased to exist. I wanted to escape from the wordless force that controlled me and imposed itself on me.
>
> I cannot say that I was lacking in courage that moment. The courage required to make a confession was a trifling matter. For one such as I, who had lived in silence for the past twenty years, the value of confession was slight indeed. People may think that I am exaggerating. But the fact is that by setting myself up the Superior's silence and refusing to confess, I had until then been experimenting with the single problem: "Is evil possible?" If I were to persist until the end in not confessing, it would prove that evil, albeit merely a petty evil, was indeed possible. But as I caught glimpses through the trees of the Superior's white skirt and white socks disappearing into the darkness of the dawn, the force that was burning in my throat became almost irresistible and I wanted to make a complete confession. I wanted to run after the Superior and cling to his sleeve and tell him in a loud voice everything that had happened on that snowy morning. It was certainly not any respect for the man that had inspired me with this wish. The Superior's force was like some strong physical power.
>
> Yet, the thought that if I should confess, the first petty evil of my life would collapse, held me back and I felt that something was tugging firmly at my back. Then the Superior's figure had passed under the main gate and disappeared under the still dark sky.
>
> Everyone was suddenly relieved and ran noisily to the front door of the temple. As I stood there absently, Tsurukawa tapped me on the shoulder. My shoulder awoke. That lean shabby shoulder of mine regained its pride.
>
> (Mishima 2001, pp. 82–83) From *The Temple of the Golden Pavilion* by Yukio *Mishima*. Published by *Secker and Warburg*. Reprinted by permission of The Random House Group Limited.

Reading this, it is tempting to conclude that the logic of moral appraisal cannot help us elucidate either strength, or weakness, of will. For there seem to be two separate characteristics of the will evaluated. Moral appraisal apparently tracks the goodness or badness, not the strength or weakness of will expressed in one's actions. Similarly, when assessing an agent's ability to stick to her plans in the face of temptation or adversity, the moral quality of these plans seems immaterial. And so, a robust distinction between strength and goodness of will would make us see the agential appraisal of both Huck and Mızogushi as unproblematic. For this appraisal would now consist of two distinct components. Hence, there would be nothing mysterious in being either weak-willed and good like Huck, or strong-willed and evil like Mizogushi.

Is this distinction sound? More specifically, does it reflect a defining feature of responsible agency or, instead, misinterpret a pair of special cases which, once correctly accounted for, confirm an implicit link between strength and goodness of will? To address these issues, I shall critically examine in Chapter 4 a recent conception of weakness of will, according to which the distinction between strength and goodness of will is both robust and fundamental.

Chapter 4

Before weakness of will

Is the link between strength and goodness of will merely contingent?[1] If so, philosophical accounts of weakness of will since the times of Plato and Aristotle would have persistently misinterpreted the phenomenon:[2] for an inherent link between strength and goodness of will is a standard assumption for them. To address this issue, I shall critically engage with Richard Holton's alternative account, which rejects this assumption as mistaken and asserts a merely contingent link between strength and goodness of will. More specifically, I shall put forth an account of akrasia as a primary failure of intentional agency and clarify how it relates to Holton's account of weakness of will that also points to a kind of failure of intentional agency, but presents this as separate from akrasia and more fundamental than it (1999, 2009, pp. 70–96). I shall argue, drawing on Aristotle's work, that the failure of intentional agency articulated by the concept of akrasia is the central case, whereas the phenomenon Holton's account is after, let us call it "ordinary weakness of will,"[3] is dependent

---

[1] This chapter substantially draws on Radoilska (2012c).

[2] Plato's and Aristotle's theories of akrasia are of major philosophical interest in their own right; furthermore, their influence can be readily felt in the current debates on this topic. *Protagoras* (Plato 2008) and *Nicomachean Ethics*, Book VII are the two main texts presenting their respective positions—the first rejecting, the second defending the possibility of akrasia. It is also well worth consulting *Republic*, Book IV (Plato 1992) which arguably sets out Plato's revised view of akrasia. The essays in Bobonich and Destrée (2007) comment on these two classical conceptions of akrasia and their ancient posterity, the focus of most contributions being Plato. Charles (1984) is an important book-length inquiry, which reconstructs Aristotle's theory within a contemporary analytic framework, a methodology already pursued in Wiggins (1979). Broadie (1994) has the merit to lay out some significant differences between the underlying assumptions of classical and contemporary approaches to weakness of will.

[3] This is to reflect Holton's central claim that his account, unlike alternatives, does justice to ordinary, untutored intuitions about weakness of will (1999, p. 241).

upon akrasia as a condition for its possibility. By this I mean that ordinary weakness of will is best understood as an unsuccessful attempt to tackle akrasia, that is, a secondary failure of intentional agency which follows and is partly explained by the primary failure it tries to redress.

The discussion proceeds as follows. I begin by outlining Holton's account of weakness of will and indicating its relevance to the present inquiry (Section 4.1). I then look into Aristotle's works to reconstruct the classical conception of akrasia, which Holton considers to be misleading (Section 4.2). Since the purpose of this analysis is not exegetical, relevant texts by Aristotle will be given close consideration; however, I shall not engage directly with the rich interpretative literature on the subject of akrasia, but selectively refer to it. In light of this analysis, I compare ordinary weakness of will with the so-called inverse akrasia discussed in Chapter 3 and identify a difficulty for Holton's proposal: to account for the negative moral appraisal it levels at weakness of will, which is presumably separate from badness of will (Section 4.3). Finally, I propose a way to address this difficulty by grounding ordinary weakness of will in the classical conception of akrasia (Section 4.4).

4.1 Holton on weakness of will

In his book *Willing, Wanting, Waiting* (2009), Holton defines what I propose to call ordinary weakness of will as follows: "unreasonable revision of a contrary inclination defeating intention (a resolution) in response to the presence of those very inclinations" (p. 78). This view is defended as an alternative to "the traditional account that identifies weakness of will and akrasia" deemed to be "not simply inadequate, but straight out wrong" (Holton 1999, pp. 243, 258). According to Holton, this fundamental error stems from the fact that, following Plato and Aristotle, many philosophers have taken peripheral cases of weakness of will to be paradigmatic and, as a result, misconceived the phenomenon at issue. More precisely, the charge is that the traditional account has focused on instances of acting against one's better judgment, which are neither representative nor difficult to account for (Holton 2003). In so doing, it has failed to appreciate the centrality of irresoluteness which comes to the fore as soon as we isolate cases of (ordinary) weakness of will without akrasia. The following vignette presents such a case:

> Christabel, an unmarried Victorian lady, has decided to embark on an affair that she knows will be disastrous. It will ruin her reputation, and quite probably leave her pregnant. Moreover, she considers it morally wrong. So she thinks it not the best option on either moral or prudential grounds. Nevertheless, she has resolved to go ahead with it. At the very last moment, however, she pulls out: not because of a rational reconsideration of the pros and cons, but because she simply loses her nerve.
>
> (Holton 1999, p. 255)

According to Holton, the interest of this vignette lies in the possibility to distinguish between, on the one hand, the traditional form of akrasia, i.e., acting against one's better judgment without ordinary weakness of will, and, on the other, ordinary weakness of will, i.e., failing to act on one's resolution without traditional weakness of will. With respect to Christabel, the locus of akrasia is to be found in her initial intention to embark on an affair, for this intention clearly goes against her better judgment. So, in Holton's terms, if she were to go ahead with her (disastrous) resolution, she would have displayed traditional akrasia but no ordinary weakness of will. In contrast, if Christabel avoids disaster by virtue of simply losing her nerve, she renders herself guilty of ordinary weakness of will, but not of akrasia.

Is this analysis persuasive? More importantly, does Christabel's vignette present a case where strength and goodness of will come apart in a way that justifies separating out two distinct phenomena, weakness of will and akrasia, the former covering failings of strength, the latter, failings of goodness of will? To address these questions, let us first look at the classical conception of akrasia, which can be found in Aristotle's philosophy.

4.2 **Aristotle on akrasia**

In this section, I shall begin to articulate the structure of the concept of akrasia as it emerges from Aristotle's discussion in the *Nicomachean Ethics* 7 and further relevant texts.[4] In doing so, my first objective will

---

[4] In the following, I shall refer to the treatise by the standard abbreviation, *EN*.

be to clarify the sense, in which akrasia can be said to involve a failure of intentional agency. For the sake of clarity, the logical form of akrasia will be outlined at the start of the discussion, which will then expand on individual features and their possible implications.

4.2.1 The logical form of akrasia

> *Akrasia is a failure of intentional agency that involves a particular kind of inner conflict, which is unnecessary in the sense that it should not have arisen in the first instance and which also gets poorly resolved; as a result, it keeps on coming back.*

This schema grounds a number of central features. *Firstly*, akrasia covers both a specific behavior and a related character disposition. *Secondly*, it is fully intelligible only from a temporarily extended perspective. *Thirdly*, a hierarchy of different kinds of values as possible ends of action is a further prerequisite for understanding akrasia. *Fourthly*, akrasia does not stem from an actual conflict between different kinds of values. *Fifthly*, the motivational conflict experienced by the akratic agent is due to his immaturity as a valuer (henceforth: evaluative immaturity). *Sixthly*, this evaluative immaturity makes akrasia an appropriate target for blame. And *seventhly*, akratic actions are best understood as pre-intentional.

Let us start to unpack this sketch of a concept by looking in some detail into the first feature, the fact that akrasia covers both a specific behavior and a related disposition (Grgic 2002). An immediate implication is that the assessment of an action as akratic cannot be done in isolation, but requires some kind of intrapersonal comparison: an akratic action is always one in a series of similar actions performed by a particular agent at different moments in time (link forth to the second feature).

This becomes clear if we think about the kind of inner conflict that characterizes akrasia (link back to the underlying schema). In *On the Soul* 3.10, it is described as a motivational conflict between two kinds of objects of attraction, the one immediately present, the other being at some distance.[5] This conflict is finally resolved in favor of the first, immediately present object. This winner is an apparent good in both senses of the word "apparent": it is conspicuous and it is not exactly what

---

[5] 433a27–b10. Henceforth, I shall employ the standard abbreviation of the title, *DA*.

it seems. Drawing on *EN* 7.4–6, things that could play such a role have to have a direct appeal to us as sentient beings, that is, to be within the resort of a natural appetite. The unmediated, essentially visceral attraction that they exercise explains both their salience and potential ambivalence. This is reflected in the underlying understanding of pleasure as an apparent good.

It is tempting to construe the second kind of object, the distant good which is the looser in the akratic contest, as more of the same in the future, a bigger reward that could be obtained by postponing immediate gratification. This is consistent with the idea that akrasia is a problem only for agents having a sense of time (second feature).[6] However, it cannot fully account for the inherent ambivalence attributed to the apparent good that the akratic goes for. Furthermore, it is at odds with the central view that akrasia is a shameful rather than just suboptimal conduct.[7] So the trouble cannot be only that akratic agents overrate present rewards. The problem seems to be deeper and more complex altogether: namely, that pleasure as unchecked appearance of the good is effectively employed as currency for selecting between separate kinds of goods. Yet, pleasure in this sense is one of the kinds to choose from and, usually, the least choiceworthy one. An important indication to this effect is given in *EN* 2.4 where the possible aims of human action are classified in connection to three different types of valuable objects: immediately pleasant, advantageous, and good without qualification.[8] Having this distinction in mind, the distant good that gets neglected because of an apparent one could belong to either of the two latter categories—advantageous or good unqualified. These include abstract and complex objects of attraction, such as intricate intellectual pursuits and collaborative activities. This suggestion is supported by the central role that the capacity of deliberative representation (phantasia bouleutikê) plays in explaining both akrasia and more successful forms of human action.[9] Hence,

---

[6] 433b5–10. On the links between preference inconsistency over time and practical irrationality, see Elster (1999).

[7] *EN* 7.4, 1148b5–7. Compare *EN* 7.1, 1145a15–17; 2, 1146a13–22; and 8, 1151a1–40.

[8] 1104b30–5a1. See also Burnyeat (1980).

[9] *DA* 3.11, 434a6–15. See also: Labarrière (1984); Canto-Sperber (2001); and Destrée (2007).

the apparent good does not have to be physically present, at hand, so to speak. It may also be immediately present to the mind's eye, because it is extremely easy to grasp as an objective as opposed to more sophisticated goals. Getting a drink versus creating a historical novel represents well this contrast. Akrasia can now be appreciated as a threat to both the scope and nature of the projects that a person can possibly pursue, not just an imprudent attitude to prospective rewards (third feature of akrasia).

Let us now turn to the core suggestion that akrasia presents an unnecessary kind of inner conflict. The thought is that the opposition between apparent and distant good stems from a distorted or, rather, underdeveloped evaluative perspective and can be avoided once this is corrected. In other words, only things that are either good without qualification or contributive to such a good can be unambiguously pleasant (Rogers 1999; Lear 2006). The conflict, experienced by akratic agents, is of their own doing. The three kinds of goods or goals of action are fundamentally compatible and could be integrated into a coherent whole, without any genuine loss. Importantly, this insight is not alien to the akratic agent who, in a way, knows what he should choose; however, this knowledge is neither actively used, nor fully integrated. *EN* 7.3 clearly expresses this idea by two complementary analogies: the knowledge of an akratic is like that we have when we are asleep; and the knowledge of beginners who know the correct conclusions, but not the argument that leads to them (Pickavé and Whiting 2008; Charles 2009). These two analogies shed further light to the ways in which the choiceworthy alternative is conceived as remote by the akratic. Firstly, its appeal is not as clear-cut. An effort is already involved in paying attention to it as the akratic accepts that this is something choiceworthy, but does not understand why. In other words, he recognizes that this is something attractive, but does not feel attracted to it. Secondly, this alternative seems much harder to obtain or realize than the apparent good. These two features make the immediate experience of the choiceworthy good uncomfortable and perhaps even unpleasant. Thus, the remoteness of the worthy objective may translate not only into motivational detachment, but also into active avoidance that plays even further in favor of the uncomplicated apparent good. An additional danger is that, by going for the apparent good, the akratic reinforces the immature evaluative stance, from which the pursuits of good and pleasure appear to be antagonistic (fourth feature of akrasia).[10]

This brings us to the point that akrasia not only starts with an unnecessary inner conflict, but also provides a poor resolution to it. A comparison with enkrateia, or self-control, helps clarify that akrasia is essentially a failure even with respect to the pursuit of immediate pleasure. As outlined in *EE* 2.8, akrasia leads to an ambivalent experience.[11] There is some pleasure associated with the consumption of the apparent good; yet, it is already then mixed with, on the one hand, anticipated displeasure for compromising one's chances to achieve the choiceworthy, but forgone good and, on the other hand, anticipated shame. The element of disappointment is built-in and this makes the akratic satisfaction fundamentally incomplete. In contrast, enkrateia provides a good resolution to the same kind of unnecessary conflict. Certainly, it is also ambivalent, because an enkratic agent regrets the unavailability of instant pleasure, whilst at the same time enjoying the right choice he makes. Yet, this motivational gap is not only easier to bridge, but also different in kind, for the enkratic has chosen the genuinely pleasant option. The frustration he experiences is just as short-lived as the akratic pleasure. This is why akrasia is deemed to be a dangerous, unhealthy character disposition, analogous to chronic illnesses of the body, whereas self-control is not (fifth feature).

The idea that akrasia provides a poor resolution to an initial motivational conflict is directly related to the fact that akratic actions, although voluntary, are not done out of choice. *EN* 7.8 points to two scenarios: according to the first, the agent goes for the apparent good on an impulse, without taking the time to properly assess the situation. Alternatively, he defects from the right course of action that was previously identified.[12] Crucial to both cases as instances of akrasia is the fact

---

[10] The notion of evaluative immaturity relates directly to that of insecure competence, introduced in the Chapter 2, see especially Section 2.2.

[11] 1224b16–22.

[12] 1151a1–40.

that that the two more demanding categories of good that get neglected for the sake of the apparent one, are within the reach of the akratic as a valuer and an agent. In other words, an akratic person is in a position to both appreciate and engage in pursuits that are either good without qualification or contributive to such pursuits. Yet, he fails to do so. This may lead to the suspicion that akrasia is not a distinctive phenomenon, but could be reduced to either fully intentional or blameless wrongdoing. In the first case, akrasia would become indistinguishable from vice; in the second—it would amount to a non-voluntary kind of behavior, which, although regrettable, cannot be attributed to the agent in a morally relevant sense. Yet Aristotle's account avoids both options. Akrasia is deemed shameful and blameworthy, but nevertheless very different from a state of moral depravity. In order to appreciate this claim, we need to look in more detail into the sixth feature of the logical form I sketched earlier, for, as we shall see in the second part of this inquiry, it is crucial that we locate correctly the focus of blame for both akrasia and related phenomena.

4.2.2 **The blameworthiness of akrasia**

Building on the preceding observations, we are in a position to see that blame does not attach to akrasia as a failure of self-mastery in the sense of being unable to carry out any plan to which the agent has previously committed, independently of whether this plan is worth pursuing or not. This becomes clear if we look again the apparent paradox posed by the so-called inverse akrasia and, more precisely, if we reflect on the issue why this paradox does not arise for the classical conception of akrasia.[13] To recall, Nomy Arpaly and Timothy Schroeder define inverse akrasia as follows (1999, p. 162):

> The most commonly discussed examples of akrasia centre around wrongdoing of one sort or another, in which desires override judgement: one is on a diet, but somehow cannot help but eat the slice of cake; one is resolved to tell an awkward truth, but somehow a lie slips out. In the cases of interest to us, however, akrasia results in what, for lack of a better word, might be called rightdoing of one sort or another. That is, the akratic course of action is superior to the course of action

---

[13] For a detailed discussion of inverse akrasia, see Chapter 2.

recommended by the agent's best judgment. Because these cases reverse our usual expectations from akratic action, we call them cases of inverse akrasia.

If what makes akrasia blameworthy is lack of self-mastery as specified earlier, instances of the phenomenon described by Arpaly and Schroeder become paradoxical, for in such instances, a person fails to act as he planned to or thought should act[14] (lack of self-mastery), yet the action is not blameworthy, but to his credit.

A possible solution is to distinguish, following Arpaly and Schroeder, between practical rationality and moral praiseworthiness and to argue that the former is not a prerequisite for the latter. Looking at Christabel's vignette, a similar route appears to be taken by Holton's account: for it locates the "stigma" attached to ordinary weakness of will in that it presents an unreasonable revision of one's intention (practical irrationality) independently of whether this intention is worthwhile carrying out on moral or even prudential grounds (praiseworthiness). I return to this vignette in Section 4.3, where I appraise the solution it points to. For now, however, let us focus on the classical conception, for which the difficulty at issue does not even arise. As indicated earlier, this has to do with the fact that the failure of intentional agency captured by the concept of akrasia is not primarily a failure of self-mastery in the sense of carrying out one's resolution, whether good or bad. This point becomes clearer, if we consider a case which is explicitly addressed by Aristotle in *EN* 7 and also credibly matches the description of inverse akrasia set out by Arpaly and Schroeder. In fact, Arpaly and Schroeder refer to it as "perhaps the earliest recorded" occurrence of inverse akrasia, in which a person "does the right thing, but does so against his best judgment" (1999, p. 162). The reference point is an episode at the center of Sophocles' tragedy *Philoctetes*, in which Neoptolemus, a young Greek prince, finds it unbearable to carry on with a dishonest stratagem, to which he has earlier consented at the insistence of his mentor, Odysseus, and has a last-minute change of heart.[15] Aristotle comments on this case

---

[14] I shall come back to the question on whether these two options are that different from each other in the concluding section of this chapter.

[15] See Chapter 2, Section 2.3 for a detailed description of the case under consideration.

both at the start and at the end of the discussion on akrasia in *EN* 7.[16] More precisely, he warns against treating akrasia and the Neoptolemus case as relevantly similar. The thought is that the analogy between the two is rather misleading. For the feature that they have in common— acting against one's better judgment or prior resolution—is insufficient to understanding the nature and significance of either phenomenon. An akratic action is at odds with the agent's correct assessment that this kind of action is ineligible on reflection. Conversely, Neoptolemus' action goes against a mistaken prior resolution. The fact that it is commendable clearly indicates that it has nothing to do with akrasia. A further reason to reject a possible concept of inverse akrasia that Aristotle points to is that it leads to confusing, sophistic claims, like the thesis that foolishness combined with akrasia amounts to virtue:

> For, because of akrasia, the person acts in the way contrary to that in which he supposes he should act; and because he supposes that good things are bad and that he should not do them, he will do good actions and not bad ones.[17]

In other words, the conjunction between practical irrationality and praiseworthiness that defines instances of inverse akrasia is excluded on Aristotle's account of akrasia, for practical irrationality and blameworthiness are two inseparable aspects of the phenomenon. This becomes clear if we relate the preceding observations to the earlier discussion on the fifth component of the conceptual schema of akrasia, evaluative immaturity, reflected by the fact that an akratic pursuit is partly defined by being an obviously wrong thing to do.[18] This brings us to the seventh and final feature of the conceptual schema drafted at the start of this chapter: the pre-intentional character of akratic agency.

---

[16] *EN* 7.2, 1146a18–22; 9, 1151b17–23.

[17] 1146a28–31.

[18] An additional indication in the same direction is offered by the contrast between akrasia in the strict sense, which is confined to plain pleasures that appeal to us as mere sentient beings, and akrasia qualified, which relates to inappropriate behavior due to more complex motivation, such as anger: cf. *EN* 7.4, 1147b23–35. These latter cases are deemed possibly excusable since the inappropriateness of the resulting behavior is not as clear-cut as in cases of akrasia unqualified. In a similar vein, Aristotle distinguishes akrasia from disproportionate attachment to otherwise worthy objectives, such as excessive interest in the well-being of one's family and friends: 1148a24–33.

4.2.3 **The pre-intentionality of akrasia**

As outlined earlier, akratic actions are voluntary but not done out of choice. This is the central feature that I propose to capture by the notion of pre-intentionality.[19] The reason for this is as follows. As indicated in *EN* 3.3, choice involves a mental state, in which both goal and corresponding course of action are fully specified and endorsed.[20] Thus understood, choice appears to be relevantly similar to intention in the demanding sense of having a plan rather than having only a goal (Bratman 1984). For entertaining and even working toward incompatible goals does not imply the kind of inner conflict that I suggested is central to the concept of akrasia. Moreover, by treating choice as a kind of intention, we are in good position to appreciate Aristotle's insistence that akrasia does not include instances, in which a person acts in accord with his choice, which itself contradicts this person's correct discernment or opinion about the right thing to do.[21] In fact, the possibility to have both correct opinions and good discernment on moral matters without acting accordingly is briefly considered in *EN* 3.2. It is then dismissed as a philosophically uninteresting case of moral depravity, whereby the agent consistently chooses unworthy options. In contrast, akrasia is deemed to present a genuine problem because it does not instantiate the agent's choice but nevertheless leads to actions that fully engage his responsibility. This problem appears particularly pressing in light of Aristotle's observation that choice is more intimately related to an agent's character than his actions and is therefore to be taken as an ultimate indicator of his moral worth.[22] Thus, in order to be persuasive, an account of akrasia as involving pre-intentional agency should be able to explain not only how it differs from vice (wrongdoing out of choice) but also from non-voluntary actions for which a person cannot be held accountable.

The schema of akrasia suggests a plausible way forward, for it points to the fact that akrasia consists of a poor resolution to an unnecessary

---

[19] On the notion of pre-intentional action, see Anscombe (1963, p. 28).

[20] 1113a10–14.

[21] Compare *EN* 7.2, 1146a13–22; and 8, 1151a20–24.

[22] 1111b5–7.

inner conflict. Both conflict and resolution can be explained by a pluralistic account recognizing that human agents act in at least two distinct ways, as indicated in *DA* 3.9–11 and *On the Movement of Animals* 6–8.[23] The first way of acting is unique to human beings. It involves capacities, such as a good-oriented volition (*boulêsis*), deliberation (*bouleusis*), discernment (*dianoia*), deliberative representation (*phantasia bouleutikê*), and choice (*proairesis*). These capacities allow human agents to exercise a considerable degree of control over their behavior. In particular, they are capable of selecting their objectives, which are merely given to non-human agents.

Yet, humans can also act in a second way, that is, as mere sentient beings. Along with other animal self-movers, they can respond directly to present incentives and orient themselves by the perceived pleasantness, or painfulness in their surroundings (Furley 1980). This more primitive mode of action is generally beneficial to human agents. It enables them to successfully perform simple and routine tasks which are better handled by instinct rather than conscious effort and planning. Moreover, the specifically human mode of action builds upon the preceding, elementary one. As indicated in the earlier discussion of *EN* 2.3, the reason for this is twofold. Firstly, perceived pleasures have stronger motivational impact on human agents than the two other sources of attraction to which they are capable to react, namely, things advantageous or good without qualification. Thus, unless properly educated, the perception of an apparent good, that is, an accessible pleasure, may lead to drastic changes in our physical condition that actually block or falsify the intuition of the two less apparent kinds of goods. Secondly, human agents mostly experience the latter through the medium of pleasant or painful experiences. Hence, anticipated pleasure may be used as an indication whether to pursue a particular kind of good or not.

This leaves us with a distinction between, on the one hand, intentional agency, which is both planning and responsive to reasons, and on the other, a rudimentary, pre-intentional kind of agency which is open to us qua sentient beings. Akrasia is clearly associated with the latter kind of

---

[23] Hereafter cited as *MA*.

agency, for it involves an unreasonable reaction to apparent incentives as opposed to reasons and not a response to invalid reasons.

An immediate objection to address is that the preceding explanation of akratic pre-intentionality, although making sense of akratic pursuits whose object is readily available, will be hard pressed to accommodate instances of akrasia where planning is apparently needed. Examples include cases, like those brought up in *EN* 7.6, where akratic agents seem to engage in strategic behavior in order to indulge their appetites. To sharpen the point of the objection: if planning is the distinguishing feature of intentional agency whereas akrasia points to a rudimentary or pre-intentional kind of agency, how are apparent instances of akratic planning to be accounted for?

MA 7 indicates a possible solution. There, Aristotle elaborates on simple, straightforward actions that do not require further planning, but immediately follow from the understanding of their respective goals, just like the conclusion of a syllogism follows from its premises. Examples are taking a walk and, perhaps more surprisingly, building a house, since this second action cannot be performed instantaneously, but is further analyzable to simpler, consecutive actions (Nussbaum 1979, p. 344).[24] Yet, the building example does not seem to be a mistake. It reappears in the discussion of intellectual virtues in *EN* 6.4 to help clarify the distinction between practical wisdom (phronêsis) and know-how (technê). Building a house is only a production, or secondary action (*poiesis*) and not an action proper (*prâxis*). It does not require the exercise of practical wisdom, or deliberation, but only know-how. This is because the kind of planning involved in the latter is purely of the means-end variety, whereas deliberation also includes considering eligible courses of action in the context of a person's broader life project. Building on this thought, it becomes apparent that planning proper is inseparable from responsiveness to reasons in the sense of identifying and successfully pursuing worthwhile ends of action. In contrast,

---

[24] Compare this with the example of making soup discussed in Chapter 2, footnote 26: although making a soup is not something we can do immediately or "at will," for it requires time and effort, it is still an elementary action in another sense.

planning that boils down to merely identifying the means to achieving an end, independently of its standing with respect to both existing commitments and potential worthwhile pursuits, is just as derivative as the kind of "practical wisdom" that some non-human animals can be said to employ in securing their survival.[25] In light of the account of akratic pre-intentionality set out earlier, instances of akratic planning clearly fit the description of the latter, derivative kind. Hence, there is no tension with the idea of akratic pre-intentionality or voluntariness without choice. More precisely, akratic pursuits that take time and effort rather than reach for instant satisfaction are consistent with the immediacy implied by the idea that akrasia presents a reaction to an incentive rather than response to a reason. This is because the relevant kind of immediacy has to do with the way in which this incentive or apparent good is pursued—without the support of deliberation or planning proper that would have put it into perspective and made it immediately clear how unworthy of pursuing this effectively is.

There is a related concern that we need to address in order to safely establish the claim that akrasia involves pre-intentional agency. This concern points to a possible tension between the proposed account of akratic pre-intentionality and the role of the so-called practical syllogism in Aristotle's explanation of akrasia.[26] For instance, it may be tempting to think that, if akratic actions can be explained as conclusions of faulty practical syllogisms, akrasia would involve a conflict of reasons, in which the invalid, yet intelligible one takes precedence over the valid, but insufficiently articulated one. If this is correct, akrasia turns out to be just as intentional as wrongdoing out of choice or moral depravity

---

[25] This concise presentation should suffice for the purposes of the present inquiry. I have developed this point in some detail elsewhere, see Radoilska (2007, pp. 272–290). On the nature and scope of practical wisdom as employed by non-human animals according to Aristotle, see Labarrière (1990).

[26] This concern could build on an interpretation, according to which the practical syllogism has two related functions in Aristotle's philosophy: the first of an explanatory tool applicable to actions in general and the second of an ideal type or model for rational actions. On the rationale for such an interpretation and its exegetical alternatives, see Corcilius (2008a, 2008b).

and, in this case, the blame that attaches to akrasia, cannot be different in kind from the blame for moral depravity as I previously suggested.

Fortunately for my argument, the tension described is only apparent and can be explained away if we look again at *MA* 7. There, a practical syllogism is employed in order to explain the possibility of voluntary action by both human and non-human animals and the paradigm case chosen is voluntary movement from one place to another. Crudely put, the model is as follows. To start with, an object is perceived (1) and if this object is subsumed under the category of either pleasant or threatening things rather than of no interest (2), and if, in addition, there is no external obstacle (3), then an action follows (4): either to try and get the thing perceived as pleasant, that is, voluntary movement toward the reference object or, conversely, to try and get away from the thing perceived as dangerous, that is, voluntary movement in the opposite direction of the reference object. Since both the occurrence and the nature of the action are determined by the conjunction of the antecedents, it is helpful to consider this necessitation by means of a syllogism whose first or major premise, the conjunction (1) and (2), reads as: "Here is an object for me to pursue/avoid" whilst the second or minor premise (3) reads as: "Nothing stops me from pursuing/avoiding this object." The conclusion (4) is an action of the following kind: trying to get/trying to get away from.

This is a credible model of purposive or pre-intentional but not planning or fully intentional action,[27] as it presents its explanandum in isolation, instead of putting it into perspective. Yet, as shown by the preceding discussion of deliberation and choice, perspectival considerations, such as timeliness and worthiness in comparison to alternative pursuits are prerequisite for fully intentional agency. In fact, the practical syllogism does not play any role in Aristotle's account of action proper (*praxis*) and is directly applied to human agency (as opposed to broader voluntary agency as in *MA* 7 above) only in the context of akrasia.

---

[27] On this distinction, see Bratman (2007, pp. 3–18). This distinction builds on the earlier contrast between having a goal and having a plan, but is not fully coextensive with it. However, possible divergences will not be given further consideration as they fall beyond the scope of the present inquiry.

4.3 **Revisiting weakness of will**

Having reconstructed the classical conception of akrasia, let us return to Christabel's vignette. In light of this reconstruction, the vignette seems to support a different conclusion from that reached by Holton.[28] As I shall aim to show in the following analysis, the vignette effectively helps challenge the contrast between traditional akrasia and ordinary weakness of will that Holton draws. Moreover, it helps identify a problematic shift of blame allocation in Holton's account of ordinary weakness of will, which, once rectified, effectively points toward a secondary failure of intentional agency dependent upon akrasia, the primary failure of intentional agency.

To clarify this critical point, let us address the issue how much of a difference there is between describing the phenomenon at issue in terms of a failed intention rather than a conflicted better judgment. Drawing on the allocation of akrasia in Christabel's case, it becomes clear that Holton takes the better judgment against which she intends to act to be motivationally inert. This understanding is also consistent with Holton's earlier remarks a propos the advantages of his proposal over the traditional view, suggesting that there is nothing special about gaps between an agent's evaluation and motivation to act and, therefore, thinking about weakness of will in terms of inner conflict is a distraction (1999, pp. 253–255). In other words, assumed here is a form of externalism about evaluative, including moral judgments. Supposing that this kind of externalism is correct, Holton is right to point out that acting against one's better judgment presents no philosophical challenge, for evaluative judgments are motivationally inert in principle. Consequently, the task at hand turns out to be explaining instances where motivation to act seems to steadily flow from an agent's evaluative judgments. This is consistent with a later paper by Holton (2003) arguing that it is strength of will rather than weakness of will that philosophers should focus their attention on.[29]

---

[28] Cf. Mele (2010) for an alternative critique which also pays particular attention to Christabel's case.

[29] The thesis Holton put forth in this paper can be summed up as follows: whilst weakness of will involves unreasonable revision of one's prior resolutions due to strong contrary

In the following, I shall not give further consideration to externalism about evaluative judgments as implied by Holton's rejection of the traditional view of akrasia. In so doing, I do not mean to suggest that it does not point to an alternative worth exploring. My reservations instead are as follows. Firstly, this kind of externalism cannot be taken for granted but needs to be argued for, however, Holton does not offer an explicit argument to this effect. Secondly, should an argument in favor of externalism about evaluative judgments prove successful, it would at the same time provide a reductionist account of akrasia along the lines I contemplated earlier, that is, not that akrasia is impossible as internalist skeptics maintain (Hare 1952; Watson 1977) but that it is all too common, provided the contingent links between evaluation and motivation. Thirdly, and most importantly, the issue addressed by the traditional view of akrasia is not about going against motivationally inert judgments. On this view, akrasia poses a challenge in need of philosophical explanation because holding a judgment that a particular course of action, A, is the best thing to do at a particular moment in time, t, is conceptually sufficient for intending to perform A at t (see, for instance, Mele 2002). Internalism about evaluative judgments offers an intuitive way of expressing this connection. However, if, following Holton, we dismiss this kind of internalism and take it that an agent's judgment in favor of A does not suffice for him to form an intention to do A at t, but requires an additional component, the akratic challenge would reappear under the guise of acting against one's intention to perform A. Following this line of thought, it turns out that ordinary weakness of will is not a different phenomenon from that addressed by the traditional view of akrasia, but merely a re-description of the same phenomenon meant to satisfy an externalist intuition about the nature of evaluative judgments.

This brings us to a second critical point I wish to make about ordinary weakness of will: the shift of blame allocation, to which this externalist re-description of akrasia leads, is problematic. Since the point of this re-description is to move away from the idea that the explanandum is

---

inclinations, strength of will involves the successful exercise of one's faculty of will-power aimed at preventing such revisions.

some sort of gap between evaluation and motivation, it becomes difficult to make sense of what the blame or, as Holton prefers to call it, the stigma (1999, pp. 253–254, 2009, p. 82) that attaches to ordinary weakness of will could even amount to. The difficulty is particularly salient in cases such as Christabel's vignette. To recap, the example is intended to work out as follows. Christabel has formed an akratic resolution but then fails to act upon it because of the very inclination, in this case, fear which this resolution was meant to offset. As a result, Christabel ends up culpable of ordinary weakness of will, that is, a failure to act upon her akratic contrary inclination defeating intention in response to pressure from this very inclination, but not of akrasia, since the resulting omission is in accord with her better judgment. But how are we to understand the point of Christabel's culpability?

As indicated earlier, Holton argues that ordinary weakness of will is blameworthy by virtue of being an unreasonable revision of a prior resolution. The blame conferring feature here is unreasonableness and, in order to fulfill its task, it has to imply an internalist picture of reasons for action. This, however, stands uneasily with the intended move away from the traditional picture of akrasia so that we begin to lose sight of what might be at stake in presumed cases of ordinary weakness of will if they are to be dissociated from akrasia.

To bring out this point, let us look again at Christabel's case. In order to be able, following Holton, to find her at fault for not acting upon her akratic resolution, we need to assume that reasons for action are generally dependent upon an agent's set plan. As long as the plan does not get revised as Holton puts it by means of "rational reconsideration of pros and cons" (1999, p. 255), it is unreasonable for the agent not to carry it out, even if this plan is in and of itself unreasonable. On this model, Christabel acts unreasonably because she does not manage to carry out her unreasonable plan, that is, she loses her nerve, and gets blamed for that.

A possible way to dissipate the ensuing air of a paradox would be to apply the distinction between internal and external reasons for action and to flesh out two separate kinds of unreasonableness at work in the earlier description. Thus, the plan Christabel set out is externally unreasonable.

The term is meant to reflect the presence of reasons that speak against the plan in question, irrespective of Christabel's endorsement of it. Another way to capture the underlying intuition is to say that it would be better if this plan did not succeed, even though Christabel might be upset. In contrast, her failure to carry out this plan is internally unreasonable. If she had not set her mind to it, there would have been nothing to reproach her for and no failure to speak of.

However, drawing on the discussion of inverse akrasia in the preceding section, there is good reason to doubt that a distinction between internal and external unreasonableness can help resolve the paradox of Christabel's culpability. To recap, instances of inverse akrasia are supposed to involve praiseworthy actions performed against an agent's better judgment at the time of action. The possibility of this kind of action implies a gap between practical irrationality, the akratic aspect of an action, on the one hand, and its blame- or praiseworthiness, on the other. The former takes as a reference point the agent's better judgment, whilst the latter reflects the moral quality of the action. Consequently, instances of inverse akrasia are praiseworthy although practically irrational.

Instances of inverse akrasia resemble Christabel's failure to act on her akratic resolution in that they also involve a "failure" of a plan, which, like Christabel's, is not worth realizing. In terms of the distinction I introduced earlier, we could say that both ordinary weakness of will without akrasia and inverse akrasia amount to internally unreasonable failures of externally unreasonable plans. This common ground between the two phenomena makes it difficult to explain why we should end up with different outcomes with respect to moral appraisal, for as indicated earlier there is reason to believe that inverse akrasia is praiseworthy, whereas, according to Holton, ordinary weakness of will is blameworthy.

A possible rejoinder could be to argue that it is a mistake to consider instances of inverse akrasia as praiseworthy.[30] I will not pursue this line of

---

[30] I have argued at some length in the Chapter 2 that these kinds of actions are indeed praiseworthy, but not akratic: for, the mental conflict these actions express is between an agent's practical and theoretical perspectives on what constitutes a good reason for action, whereas the mental conflict that defines akrasia takes place within the agent's practical perspective on reasons for action.

reasoning here because even if the rejoinder is successful, this will not suffice to make sense of Christabel's culpability. In essence, although unworthy of praise, instances of inverse akrasia would still be blameless. This is an intuitive way to make room for the feature of inverse akrasia that underpins the claim about its praiseworthiness. This feature has to do with the fact that inverse akratic actions although performed against the agent's better judgment are still performed for a reason. This reason may not be fully appreciated or even articulated by the agent, yet, it clearly figures within his motivational set. To use Bernard Williams's helpful expression, there is a "sound deliberative route," following which the agent could counterfactually acknowledge the reason upon which he acts as his better judgment (Williams 1981). If this is correct, the reason at issue is not an external one. Consequently, the ensuing inverse akratic action is not only an externally reasonable one, but also an internally reasonable one. We may be reluctant to praise inverse akratic agents since, although they do the right thing, they do not do so wholeheartedly. However, we cannot deny the fact that they do the right thing intentionally, that is, for a reason that they are aware of.

This is bad news for Christabel's culpability, for in her case the plan she "fails" to carry out is clearly not only externally but also internally unreasonable, for it is, as Holton points out, an akratic resolution. The upshot is that the overriding reasons against going ahead with the affair are not merely counterfactually accessible to Christabel but have effective purchase on her. This is indeed the point of her trying to form an akratic resolution—being able to resist these compelling reasons. In light of this, Christabel's "merely losing her nerve" looks like a very good response to the reasons at issue, for she is correct to be afraid of going ahead with the affair and, unlike inverse akratic agents, she is equally aware of being correct.[31] Since there is no defensible sense, in which we could say that what Christabel ended up doing was unreasonable, ordinary weakness of will without akrasia turns out to be blameless.

---

[31] Again, as argued in Chapter 2, what goes awry in inverse akrasia is the agent's second-order reflection on her reasons for action, i.e., her moral self-appraisal is incorrect. This, however, does not undermine the agent's first-order awareness of these reasons as being her reasons for action.

The preceding analysis has two related implications. The first is that Holton's account of ordinary weakness of will implicitly relies on a kind of internalism about reasons for action that is also at the heart of the traditional view of akrasia. As a result, it becomes impossible to note any significant difference between the two views. The second is that, by reverting to the internalist premises it sought to avoid, Holton's account of ordinary weakness of will is bound to tell conflicting stories about the relationship between motivation and evaluation, internal and external reasons for action.

Does this mean that we should abandon the notion of ordinary weakness of will and, if so, would this not be equally damaging to the classical conception of akrasia reconstructed in the previous section? For, like Holton's it also points to a failure of intentional agency rather than conflicted better judgment like the traditional view. In the remainder of this chapter, I shall aim to address both issues. More precisely, I shall argue that there is a distinct phenomenon that Holton's account has the merit to point to and that this phenomenon is best understood as a secondary failure of intentional agency. By clarifying the significance of this failure, we are in a position to both anticipate concerns about the conception of akrasia defended here and bring into relief the way in which it integrates internal as well as external constraints on reasons for action.

4.4 Weakness of will as a failure to resist akrasia

The classical conception of akrasia as primary failure of intentional agency reconstructed in Section 4.2 provides support for a (moderately) revised account of ordinary weakness of will. In particular, it helps straighten up the story about blame allocation for ordinary weakness of will and, as a result, makes it possible to safely distinguish the latter from the phenomenon the traditional view of akrasia is after. To recap, the classical conception articulates akrasia in the following way. Akrasia is a primary failure of intentional agency in the sense that it involves a motivational conflict which is only due to the akratic agent's evaluative immaturity and not to some conflict of values. The blameworthiness of akrasia reflects the pre-intentional status of akratic wrongdoing. More specifically, it brings into focus the fact that akratic pursuits are obviously ineligible on reflection and, in this sense, akratic agents fail to put two and two together. As we saw earlier, this feature of akrasia is indispensable for explaining why the problem of inverse akrasia does not arise for the classical conception. In terms of the distinction between internal and external unreasonableness, akratic actions can be said to not only exhibit both, but in a way, to precede the very possibility to distinguish between these kinds of unreasonableness. This is because the failure involved in akrasia is that to engage in fully intentional agency instead of taking one's cue from what is immediately present like a mere purposive agent. In this sense, akrasia is a primary failure of intentional agency.

Drawing on this conception, it becomes apparent that ordinary weakness of will can be explained as a secondary failure of intentional agency, that is, a failure to tackle the problem posed by akrasia. In this respect, the contrary inclination defeating intention or resolution, as Holton puts it, which gets overturned in instances of ordinary weakness of will, can be usefully compared to unsuccessful pre-commitment (Elster 1984, 2000). Interestingly, Holton considers the possibility of such a connection, but then dismisses it, because he believes that third-party involvement, as in the original story of Ulysses and the Sirens, is central to pre-commitment but inessential to the phenomenon he aims to clarify (Holton 1999, pp. 245–246). However, if we take third-party involvement to be one way of improving the prospects of certain pre-commitments rather than a distinctive feature of the underlying intention,[32] the similarities between resolution and pre-commitment become apparent. Firstly, they are both future-oriented. By this I mean that they take the following logical form: at a moment in time, t_1 an agent forms the intention to perform an action when a subsequent moment in time, t_2 takes place.[33] Secondly, both are meant to ensure that, when t_2 arrives, the agent sticks to the plan

---

[32] The subsequent discussion of pre-commitment draws on Radoilska (2012a).

[33] Alternatively, the logical form could be presented as involving counterfactuals, that is, in a situation s_1 an agent forms the intention to perform an action should another situation, s_2, arise. Nothing of significance for the present argument hangs on whether we choose the one or the other way of presenting pre-commitment/resolution.

he formed at t_1. These two features are closely connected so that there is no need for extra reason, other than the lapse of time between t_1 and t_2, for an agent to be concerned about his sticking to the plan. In this sense, pre-commitment can be seen as a paradigm, albeit inconspicuous case of intentional agency.

In contrast, in order for pre-commitment to come to the fore, an extra reason is required. Examples include forms of self-binding, to which Elster (1984) first drew attention, as well as contrary inclination defeating intentions as defined by Holton (1999). The common ground the two kinds of planning share is that at t_1 the agent anticipates, as a part of the planning, various kinds of difficulties that are likely to jeopardize his undertaking at t_2. In the case of contrary inclination defeating intentions, these difficulties have to do with motives that the agent would like to be rid of. In light of the preceding critical discussion of ordinary weakness of will, it is persuasive to attribute the drawbacks concerning blame allocation and distinctiveness vis-à-vis the traditional view of akrasia to under-describing the phenomenon at issue. The alternative view presented here fills in the missing part of the story. In particular, it depicts the circumstance of ordinary weakness of will as involving one's realization of being in the way of akrasia, coupled with ambition to extricate oneself by means of pre-commitment. In other words, there is a primary failure of intentional agency that a person sets to resolve by means of fully intentional agency. However, since akrasia covers both a specific behavior and an underlying character disposition (the first feature of the conceptual schema I outlined in Section 4.2), the circumstance of ordinary weakness of will is more likely than not to give rise to actual cases of ordinary weakness of will, that is, secondary failures of intentional agency. This is because of the immediate salience of akratic distractions, which can be experienced as irresistible in the grips of akrasia, independently of the agent's prior resolution to resist such distractions. Following this line of thought, it becomes apparent that the seeds of failure involved in ordinary weakness of will are already sown by the initial failure it aims to resolve, that is, akrasia.

By grounding the revised account of ordinary weakness of will in a conception of akrasia as primary failure of intentional agency, we are able to address the drawbacks of the original account as well as maintain the compelling intuition at the heart of Holton's proposal, according to which "the central cases of weakness of will are best characterized not as cases in which people act against their better judgment, but as cases in which they fail to act on their intentions" (1999, p. 241). Moreover, we are in a position to appreciate the sense, in which weakness of will understood as secondary failure of intentional agency, can be seen as more "ordinary" than akrasia from a phenomenological or experiential viewpoint, although the latter is conceptually fundamental, for it is the secondary failure to tackle the primary, pre-intentional one that brings the scope of the underlying problem into focus. In this respect, it is plausible to consider that more often than not the experience of akrasia goes hand in hand with that of ordinary weakness of will.

Where does this leave us with respect to our original query: Is the link between strength and goodness of will merely contingent? By integrating Holton's notion of ordinary weakness of will into the classical conception of akrasia, we were able to show that the link between these two features of the will cannot be contingent. Yet, we have not yet defined what this link amounts to. This is the task I shall aim to complete in Chapter 5.

Addiction and weakness of will: An integrated account

The preceding chapters identified a conundrum about the possibility of a general theory of responsibility and explored its implications for understanding weak-willed and addiction-centered agency. This conundrum has the following shape. Each of the approaches discussed—volitional (in Chapter 1) and non-volitional (in Chapters 2 and 3)—is meant to offer a comprehensive account of responsibility. Yet, the resulting accounts are well equipped to tackle some central cases, but not others. In particular, no account has been able to conceptualize satisfactorily both weakness of will and addiction. A possible explanation of this upshot (Shoemaker 2011) is that volitional and non-volitional accounts, such as Wallace (1994), Smith (2005), and Arpaly (2003), are after separate target concepts rather than alternative conceptions of the same concept of responsibility. Having considered this explanation in some detail (in Chapter 2), it becomes apparent that a more promising alternative is to formulate a more fundamental conception of responsibility which can integrate insights from the volitional and non-volitional conceptions and explain their apparent disagreements. This is because both volitional and non-volitional conceptions aim to answer the same kind of questions and to address related concerns, an unlikely scenario if they were to flesh out separate responsibility concepts, such as attributability, accountability, and answerability. By formulating a third, more fundamental conception of responsibility, we are also able to offer an integrated account of the phenomena of weakness of will and addiction, and their respective import on responsible agency, building on the Aristotelian account of akrasia developed in Chapter 4.

5.1 **Action as actualization**

A first step in this direction is to identify and explore the models of morally relevant or responsible action implied by alternatives conceptions. "Action" will be employed here in a broad sense to include attitudes: they are something an agent develops, expresses, etc. Building on a distinction between separate models of action proposed by Shapiro (2001),[1] we can see that volitional accounts conceive responsible action in terms of production, while non-volitional accounts conceive it in terms of assertion.[2] On the first model, the point of action is to bring about an effect. Voluntary control over the production of this effect is essential, if the agent is to be held responsible for it. On the second model, the point of action is to assert the agent's evaluative stance. A reflective commitment to this stance is clearly more significant than control over the means of assertion. This explains why voluntary control appears as central on volitional accounts, but peripheral on non-volitional ones. It also enables us to appreciate that these accounts are not mutually exclusive. For the models of action they build on are not mutually exclusive: many responsible actions assert the agent's evaluative stance by bringing about some effect.

This speaks in favor of a more fundamental model of action which, to acknowledge the Aristotelian inspiration of this project, I would like to

---

[1] Shapiro (2001) distinguishes between three models of action in order to explain some disagreements within normative ethical theory and to clarify the interest of Kantian constructivism. The tripartite distinction on offer here is not meant to map onto that proposed by Shapiro. The two projects occupy different levels of analysis, normative ethics, and moral psychology. More importantly, they serve different objectives: as indicated earlier in the discussion (see, for instance, Chapter 2, Section 2.4) the Aristotelian theory of responsible agency that is developed here aims to be comprehensive by reconciling aspects of constructivist, as well as recognitional views of practical reason in general and reasons for action in particular. And so, I take the model of action championed in Shapiro (2001), action as participation, which is constructivist, to be less fundamental than the Aristotelian model of action as actualization that will be defended here.

[2] Two non-volitional accounts were critically examined in earlier chapters: Smith's rational relations, and Arpaly's quality-of-will view. The model discussed here, action as assertion, is meant to cover the presuppositions that both alternatives share in common qua non-volitional accounts. Thus, although I am prepared to acknowledge that action as expression could be a better fitting label with respect to Arpaly's view, since this view aims to go beyond the articulate or consciously held evaluative judgments of agents to include their whole motivational sets, nothing of significance hangs on this choice of nomenclature.

call action as actualization. Here is an example: by writing well, a person becomes and continues to be a good writer (assertive aspect) and the works she creates are good (productive aspect). As the example clearly shows, the actualization model offers a seamless common ground for the appraisal of both assertive and productive aspects of an action. In so doing, it indicates a possible solution to the conundrum about the possibility of a general theory of responsibility recalled at the start of this section. This is because the actualization model supports a more fundamental notion of agential control which applies equally to the productive and assertive aspects of an action. And so, it becomes possible to uphold both the parity of actions and attitudes as objects of moral appraisal and the important intuition according to which it is unfair to hold a person responsible for things that are not up to her, the two theoretical desiderata that jointly define a good answer to the underlying question motivating the present inquiry: What is the best way to conceptualize responsibility?

Before expanding on the implications of the actualization model to addressing outstanding issues about addiction and weakness of will, I shall say more about the Aristotelian background of the proposed conceptualization.[3] This would make clearer the difference between the notion of agential control supported by the actualization model and that of voluntary control supported by the production model.

Aristotle's theory of action allows for two kinds of actions: productions (actions as doings) and actions proper (actions as self-actualizations or coming to being). Unsurprisingly, productions are conceived as derivative actions, the point of which is to facilitate actions proper. Naturally, this is not to say that actions proper are not supposed to produce any effects in the world. Instead, the idea is that, in addition to this productive

---

[3] The following discussion is not meant as a comprehensive exposé of Aristotle's theory of action, let alone a scholarly contribution to the vast exegetical literature on the topic. Instead, the ambition is to articulate the sense in which the proposed conception is in continuity with a fecund philosophical tradition, Aristotelianism, whilst at the same time being an original contribution to a contemporary debate. Having said that, the outline of Aristotle's views on action here I based on Radoilska (2007), a monograph in which I engage more closely both with ancient sources and alternative scholarly interpretations of Aristotle's works in the recent literature.

aspect, the achievement of an external end, actions proper are also ends in themselves, that is to say, the performance of such actions is already an achievement in itself, independently of whether they also manage to bring about a desirable outcome or not. In other words, productions are incomplete actions rather than actions proper being unproductive.

To appreciate the distinctive feature of actions proper as worthwhile in their own right, not only as pursuits of further valuable ends beyond their very performance, let us consider an analogy. Virtue, like literary talent, is a virtual, as opposed to actual moral viz. aesthetic worth, a good "in potentia" only that calls to be brought into the world.

Arguably, this analogy holds true of responsible agency broadly conceived. For on Aristotle's account human beings are incomplete in a way that no other biological species is, and this is because of their capacity for rational agency. They have the unique task to make themselves up on the go, as it were, through their actions. Hence, the so-called Function argument, which is often taken to show how incorrigibly essentialist Aristotle's philosophy is, does in fact indicate the opposite—a space, and a need for active involvement in order to become a person, an actual human being with a history and character of his or her own, a member of the moral community, fit to both give and receive moral appraisal, to engage in and be the target of the full range of participant reactive attitudes, including praise and gratitude, resentment and blame.[4] We may, of course, refer to this actualization as self-creation as long as we do not get muddled with the idea of a self-creation practically ex nihilo that was put forth by the twentieth-century existentialists, such as Sartre (2003, 2007). In contrast, on an Aristotelian picture, actualization is made possible by constitutive constraints: a human being can only become a person, a moral agent of some character or other, or indeed fail to do so. Thus, actualization is best understood as self-fulfillment, an exercise of natural autonomy rather than an act of self-creation.

---

[4] The Function argument can be found in *Nicomachean Ethics* 1.2. As indicated earlier, the argument is often taken to represent a form of naturalistic fallacy, whereby "human flourishing" and the corresponding "duties of a human being" are inappropriately derived from "human nature." For an explanation why this is not the case, see Radoilska (2007, pp. 233–254).

To illustrate what I mean by "natural autonomy," let us briefly consider the first known application of the word "autonomy" to a human being. In Sophocles' tragedy *Antigone*, the Chorus reproaches the main character for burying the body of her brother whom the polis has decided to deny a burial for being a traitor. In so doing, they ask Antigone whether she takes herself to be "autonomous" viz. in a position to give herself a law. The point made by the Chorus is that only the polis, the body of citizens jointly can appropriately undertake such self-legislative function. By deciding what is right and wrong on her own, regardless of her city's will, Antigone commits an act of hubris, the pivotal fault that turns an otherwise good character into a tragic hero. So, unlike Antigone's tragic autonomy, natural autonomy is a law that recognizes the "self" it emanates from and applies to for what it is instead of trying to turn it into something else. It perfects, instead of destroying this self.

Thus, natural autonomy is best conceived in contrast to arbitrariness and artificiality: unlike artifacts, natural things are ends in themselves. By implication, the natural autonomy of human beings, whom Aristotle famously defined as both "rational" and "political," would be at odds with the unlimited, and meaningless, control that is implied by Sartrean self-creation. Human beings speak a language. They live in a community of agents, whose task is to make it possible that every agent can—both individually and jointly with others—engage in meaningful self-actualization.

This Aristotelian way of grounding our capacity for rational agency in living together with others is far from being constructivist, let alone metaphorical. Consider, for instance, courage and justice, two virtues of necessity, as Aristotle dubs them in the *Politics* 7.13–15 for their exercise is called for because others are being threatening and unjust with respect to us or third parties. What is more, even unbound or free virtues, such as friendship, and the virtues of the intellect in general are also dependent on others' appreciation of and willingness to support, if not to take part in, their actualization. Natural autonomy at the heart of the actualization model is both more visceral and down-to-earth than constructivist alternatives.[5]

---

[5] See, however, Korsgaard (2008) for an interesting constructivist approach which also integrates some aspects of Aristotle's theory of action.

By conceiving virtues as ethical or aesthetic or epistemic etc. values *in potentia* that only come to life through actions proper, the actualization model is able to show how agential control and self-control are intimately entwined in a way that the production model fails to grasp. For it construes the notion of voluntary control as one-directional dependence from agent to world as though the only point of self-control in action is to back up control over the effects of this action. Yet as the parity of actions and attitudes as legitimate objects of moral appraisal established throughout this inquiry points to, agential control might be best understood in terms of interdependence, a dialectic shaping both action and agent. The actualization model provides us with a non-mysterious way to conceptualize this interdependence: through the exercise of control over things in the world we not only learn how to exercise self-control in action. Being repeatedly successful or unsuccessful in this respect leads to us developing certain dispositions which in turn make the future exercise of self-control with respect to some actions either superfluous or futile. As we shall see in the subsequent sections, this final point will prove of great significance for disentangling addiction and weakness of will from other forms of less than successful, yet responsible agency.

5.2 **Success in action and the guise of the good**

Catching a train, getting a drink of water, greeting an acquaintance—every intentional action is a form of success, that of doing what one is minded to do. This basic form of success in action is different from another, more conspicuous one, to which it is often assimilated—bringing about a desired outcome. Yet these two forms of success may easily come apart even in the simplest of actions: a person boards the wrong train, or gets a drink of water which happens to be poisonous, or puts an acquaintance in an awkward situation by greeting her, instead of being civil. In all three cases the agent does as intended, but fails to bring about the intended outcome. Alternatively, the agent could bring about the intended outcome and yet fail to do as intended: a person ends up drinking water as planned in spite of akratically ordering wine, for, as it turns out, there is nothing but water to be had on this train. A third form of success becomes apparent when we look at intentional actions as more or less appropriate answers to the question of what an agent should do. This question brings together a variety of considerations, including: the significance of individual actions in the context of a person's commitments, projects and obligations, the demands others can reasonably address to her, and the constraints under which she has to act. As in the previous cases, being successful at answering the question of what one should do does not imply, nor is it implied by, success in either doing what one is minded to do or bringing about a desired outcome: catching the right train could still be a wrong thing to do, just as a failure to get on it as planned could be an act of courage, all the more admirable for being unplanned.

In light of these remarks, we can see that with respect to actions "less than successful" could have a very specific meaning, denoting actions that are successful in one or other, but not all three ways identified earlier. So, when I wrote at the end of the previous section that addiction and weakness of will are distinctive kinds of less than successful, though responsible agency I was applying in anticipation the term of art just introduced.

Less than successful actions are rather difficult to spot on the production and assertion models. For each of these models attempts to tackle the variety of success in action by reducing alternatives to the one success form which best fits the kind of action it takes to be fundamental. On the production model, success in action adds up to bringing about an intended outcome. Conversely, on the assertion model, a successful action is a good answer to the question of what the agent should do on a specific occasion. By being reductive, both approaches fail to capture the complexity of success in action. As a result, they tend to recast instances of less than successful agency, including weakness of will and addiction, either as wholly unsuccessful to the point of raising the question whether intentional agency has even taken place, or as wholly successful to the point of losing sight of what makes these phenomena perplexing not only to an informed observer, but more importantly to the agent herself.

In contrast, the actualization model is able to do justice to the variety, and complexity, of success in action. For it is not meant to replace the two other models, but to integrate them into a unified picture of responsible agency—unified, though not homogenous. The third form of success in action, doing what one is minded to do, which the actualization model brings into relief, is more fundamental than the other two—bringing about an intended outcome and answering well the question of what one should do by acting in a particular way. What makes it more fundamental, however, is that it offers a common ground linking the two less central forms of success in action; it does not supersede them.

This triadic structure of success in action is borne out of the phenomenology of intentional agency. In most ordinary cases, such as catching a train, getting a drink of water, and greeting an acquaintance success in action would cover all three senses: if successful, an agent would typically bring about a desired outcome by doing what she is minded to do and her doing so would be a fair answer to the general question of what she should do. It takes a thought experiment, like the examples at the start of this section, to disentangle these forms of success even at the level of one-step everyday actions. A major advantage of the actualization model is that it can explain both why the expectation that a successful action amounts to achievement in all three senses is legitimate and how some intentional actions may nevertheless frustrate this expectation by being less than successful, though not entirely unsuccessful.

The expectation at issue may be formulated as follows.

(1) At its very basic, success in action involves two things: (i) an agent's trying to achieve or get something done; and (ii), her endeavor coming to fruition.

(2) The possibility of different forms of success in action gets introduced with the second element, a success condition that may be specified in different ways.

(3) However, the first element is what makes success in action itself possible, and that is intending.

(4) Looking back at intending from its point of completion, which is success in action, it becomes clear that:
Intending is just acting under the guise of the good: trying to achieve something is to aim at success in achieving it.

The expectation turns out to a version of the thesis that intending or pursuing an end implies perceiving it as good in some respect—hence, the term "the Guise of the Good," by which it is frequently referred to following Velleman (1992).[6]

The Guise of the Good seems to be at odds with the idea that weak-willed actions are performed against one's better judgment. It also seems at odds with the view of addiction-centered agency sketched earlier in this book: for, on this view, addiction involves persisting with some pursuits that the agent no longer considers as good in any respect, that is, not even pleasant (De Quincey 2002, ch. 2). This apparent tension is typically resolved in one of the following ways: the first is to argue that the Guise of the Good offers a misleading model of intentional action, to which weakness of will provides a clear counterexample; the second is to show that weakness of will is consistent with the Guise of the Good. Stocker (1979) and Velleman (1992) are examples of the former strategy, Tenenbaum (2007) and Raz (2011) of the latter. The point of contention is whether perceiving what one attempts to achieve as good in some respect goes beyond a minimal, purely analytic understanding of "good" that is already contained in the notion of achievement as something worth achieving viz. something worth the agent's while viz. something that the agent considers as valuable or good in some respect. Contesters of the Guise of the Good have no quarrel with this minimal, and uninformative, interpretation. What they want to deny that the Guise of the Good establishes a more robust or substantive link between intending something and judging it to be worth doing viz. good in some respect. For instance, Stocker (1979, p. 744) voices the challenge of interest to us in the following way:

> Through spiritual or physical tiredness, through accidie, through weakness of body, through illness, through general apathy, through despair, through inability

---

[6] Following Garcia (1990), I will assume that intending is more fundamental than acting with an intention and acting intentionally and so will use the term "intending" to cover both. This is because a distinction between intentions preceding actions and intentions embedded in actions is not central for the version of the Guise of the Good defended here, for I take it that the thesis should cover both. See, however, Raz (2011, ch. 4) for a strategy which heavily relies on this distinction to qualify the Guise of the Good as applicable only to some, but not all intentions.

to concentrate, through a feeling of uselessness or futility, and so on, one may feel less and less motivated to seek what is good. One's lessened desire need not signal, much less be the product of, the fact that, or one's belief that, there is less good to be obtained or produced, as in the case of a universal Weltschmertz. Indeed, a frequent added defect of being in such 'depressions' is that one sees all the good to be won or saved and one lacks the will, interest, desire, or strength.

To recap, Stocker's challenge to the Guise of the Good, substantively interpreted, is that perceiving an end as worthwhile or good may easily coexist with no intention to pursuing it. By contrast, Velleman (1992, pp. 21–22) construes the challenge looking from the opposite side of the contested relationship, intentions in the absence of positive evaluation:

> Being in despair doesn't prevent me from being moved to act, however. I am moved to stay at home, refuse all invitations, keep the shades drawn, and privately curse the day I was born. I may even be moved to smash some crockery, though not in order to feel better, mind you, since trying to feel better seems just as ludicrous a project as any other. (Someone who smashes crockery in order to feel better didn't feel all that bad to begin with.) What's more, I engage in these actions not only out of despair but also in light of and on the grounds of despair. That is, despair is part of my reason as well as part of my motive for acting. But do I regard my actions, in light of my despair, as good or desirable or positive things to do? Far from it. I am determined never to do a good or desirable or positive thing again.

These two lines of critique, Stocker's and Velleman's, are often considered in the literature as representing two separate challenges leveled at the same target, the Guise of the Good. For instance, in his response to the challenges, Tenenbaum (2007) takes it that they refer to different categories of actions posing different kinds of difficulties for a proponent of the Guise of the Good: accidie and akrasia. While instances of the former, in tune with Stocker's eloquent description, are defined by a kind of perplexing inability to pursue what one clearly appreciates as worth pursuing, instances of the latter, in tune with Velleman's vignette, are pursuits undertaken in the knowledge of their worthlessness, if not in virtue of their being so disvalued.

Tenenbaum's reply to the former challenge is to show that the Guise of the Good can make sense of accidie. In a nutshell, although agents affected by accidie appreciate some pursuits as worthwhile, they do not appreciate any pursuit of theirs as worthy of success. And so, accidie proves consistent with the Guise of the Good. Cast in the terms of the thesis that flow from the actualization model, the solution takes the following form: since an agent in a state of accidie does not aim at success in achieving anything, she does not try to achieve anything. Intending is absent, for no valuing takes place from the agent's first-personal or practical as opposed to her internalized third-personal or reflective perspective.[7]

Similarly, Tenenbaum's reply to the latter challenge is to show that the Guise of the Good can also integrate akrasia. In essence, akratic agents have a merely oblique, or indirect cognition of the value of the course of action that they judge to be better; what's more, their considered judgment is overturned under the influence of a more vivid and immediate, although misleading appearance of value. In other words, akratic intending is still acting under the guise of the good, albeit a confused one.

Tenenbaum's dual reply has the merit to point out that the Guise of the Good does not have to state a straight and simple link between intending and valuing in order to count as a substantive, informative claim about the psychology of action. For nothing in the thesis itself justifies the expectation of uniform simplicity throughout the domain of intentional viz. responsible agency so that even Satan should turn out to be sappy, to paraphrase Velleman's charge against an influential earlier statement of the Guise of the Good (Anscombe 1963). However, by responding separately to Stocker (1979) and Velleman (1992), Tenenbaum fails to acknowledge that these two lines of argument are intimately related and refer to the same cluster of cases, which I termed earlier less than successful actions. For these cases often combine both sides of the challenge: intending without valuing and valuing without intending. In particular, disvaluing what one pursues while valuing what one doesn't is a fair account of the phenomenology of both akrasia and addiction. And so, a successful response to the Stocker–Velleman challenge should explain how these two sides of less than successful agency may coexist under the guise of the good. I turn to this task in Section 5.3.

---

[7] On the distinction between these two perspectives, see Chapter 3, Section 3.3. I say more about accidie and its relationship to depression in Radoilska (2013a).

5.3 **Less than successful actions**

To capture the nature and significance of this category of actions, let us first consider Aristotle's solution to a related puzzle which flows from adopting a substantive version of the Guise of the Good, like the one implied by the actualization model. This puzzle becomes apparent when we look more closely at the term of "good" in the Guise of the Good: Does it refer to a purely subjective, first-personal evaluation on the part of the agent at the time of action? Alternatively, does it have to equally pass some further test, such as being worthwhile from a third-personal perspective, be it an informed observer's, or the agent's own reflective stance? In Aristotle's terms: is it the good itself or merely an appearance of the good that constitutes the proper end or object of wish that motivates action?

Here is Aristotle's suggestion:

> . . . absolutely and in truth the good is the object of wish, but for each person the apparent good; that which is in truth an object of wish is an object of wish to the good man, while any chance thing may be so to the bad man, as in the case of bodies also the things that are in truth wholesome are wholesome for bodies in good condition, while for those that are diseased other things are wholesome—or bitter or sweet or hot or heavy, and so on; since the good man judges each class of things rightly and, and in each the truth appears to him. For each state of character has its own ideas of the noble and the pleasant, and perhaps the good man differs from others most by seeing the truth in each class of things, being as it were the norm and measure of them. In most things the error seems to be due to pleasure; for it appears a good when it is not. We therefore choose the pleasant as good, and avoid pain as evil.
>
> (*Nicomachean Ethics* 3.4)

By bringing together the subjective and objective perspectives on "good" in the Guise of the Good, Aristotle's suggestion has direct implications for defining success in action and especially for establishing the scope of less than successful actions. In particular, it enables us to flesh out the intuitive, yet elusive link between intending and valuing as a distinctive kind of future-oriented desirability judgment whose logical form is laid bare in the sentence-type of the Latin textbook example: Delenda est Carthago. Unsurprisingly, the standard translation—"Carthage must be destroyed"—does not do justice to the form of thought of interest to us: we do not have an exact equivalent of the passive periphrastic, the grammatical structure that underpins the example. The urgency of the specified action that this structure communicates is not that of sheer necessity or a "must." Instead, it derives from a judgment recognizing an object as being of a certain kind, such as to require specific action to be taken by anyone who makes that judgment. And so, the judgment under consideration is clearly not a theoretical one: it is either a statement of plan or invitation for action. To return to the Carthage example for illustration: the Phoenician city, which is the object of judgment, is recognized as so powerful that its sheer existence poses a threat. The fact that the basis of judgment, Carthage being powerful, is not explicitly mentioned in the example is immaterial since the suggestion that Carthage be destroyed is clearly presented as a natural consequence of its being the kind of city that merits destruction. What is more, it is also presented as a forthcoming event, something bound to happen: the gerundive "delenda" functions here as a future participle suggesting not only the fittingness of Carthage's destruction, but also its imminence. Yet, this is not a probability judgment: Carthage will not destroy itself. The future participle is passive indicating the need for action and for an agent who commits to bringing about the desired event, the destruction of Carthage. Who should this agent be? Anyone who recognizes Carthage as the kind of city whose destruction is called for, anyone who makes or agrees with the distinctive future-oriented desirability judgment expressed in "Delenda est Carthago."

With the Carthage example in mind, let us return to Aristotle's solution to the apparent tension between subjective and objective interpretations of "good" in the Guise of the Good. Judging what is good or worth pursuing defines the agent just as much as it defines the course of her intended action: success in action presupposes that assertion and production come together. This natural link between valuing and intending also explains why the question of what an agent should do is not extraneous to assessing whether her actions are intentional: on its own, bringing about a desirable outcome is insufficient to account for a fully successful action or, for that matter, a less than successful one. For instance, if Carthage is not the kind of city whose destruction is called for, committing to the judgment Delenda est Carthago is not going to lead to success in action. Although the Romans did eventually succeed in destroying Carthage and so they did bring about the desired outcome, once achieved, its utter undesirability became apparent: what was meant to mark Rome's glorious triumph over a long-standing ferocious enemy went down in history as an example of callous cruelty.

This, however, is not the kind of less than successful agency that is involved in addiction and weakness of will. In addition to being mistaken about what they should do, weak-willed agents and addicts are at least dimly aware of making the mistake that they make. What's more, in the central and most problematic cases, that is, akrasia as primary failure of intentional agency analyzed in Chapter 4, this mistake is committed with eyes wide open. In these latter cases, intending without valuing is inseparable from valuing without intending. And, in light of the triadic structure of success in action that the actualization model brings into relief, we are able to detect a loose connection that forms between intending and valuing even in these instances of strict or clear-eyed akrasia so as to spur purposive action. This is due to the entanglement of two concomitant desirability judgments which seem able to cancel out one another's obvious deficiencies: intending without valuing and valuing without intending. Yet, as argued earlier (see Chapter 4), akrasia is a poor resolution of an unnecessary conflict. We are now in a position to say more about why this is so: akratic actions are successful in terms of production to the exact degree that they are unsuccessful in terms of assertion. For an akratic action is not just an achievement that one disvalues, but something achieved in virtue of being disvalued. Akratic actions are necessarily less than successful actions.

This specificity of akrasia helps put into perspective skepticism about it being compatible with fully intentional agency, which might have been prompted by the earlier claim that akrasia is a primary failure of intentional agency. This skeptic impression derives from the entanglement between successful production and unsuccessful assertion that constitutes an akratic action. For in central cases at least this entanglement makes it impossible to tell whether the agent is actually doing what she is minded to do—impossible not just for an observer but crucially for the agent herself. Nevertheless, success in action is the norm, not the mark of intending. Being necessarily less than successful, akratic actions are rightly considered derivative, even parasitic with respect to actions whose success is a genuine possibility. This, however, does not preclude them from being sufficiently intended as to call for full-blown moral appraisal, well within the limits of responsible agency.

5.4 Concluding remarks: The offspring of akrasia

Having articulated the structure of akratic actions as necessarily less than successful, I will now aim to show that this structure also applies, mutatis mutandis, to addiction and not only weakness of will. To do so, let us first take stock of the puzzles about addiction we ended up with while trying to make sense of addiction-centered agency from either a volitional or a non-volitional perspective (see Chapters 1 and 2). In essence, these puzzles divide into two kinds: uncertainty about the boundaries of intentional viz. responsible agency, on the one hand, and conflicting intuitions about the wrongness of addiction, on the other. The first kind of puzzles derives from the idea that a degree of compulsion is a defining feature of addictive behaviors. At first blush, this idea generates the following plausible conclusion: compulsion diminishes control over one's actions; therefore, it warrants at least partial excuse for addictive behaviors (Wallace 1994, 1999). Yet, a closer look at the phenomenology of addictive behavior, as well as first-personal memoirs of people with addiction clearly indicates that addictions are rarely unmanageable (Ainslie 2001; Wurtzel 2002). Not only are cues rarely irresistible; more importantly, addiction-motivated behavior is compatible with successful planning (Levy 2006). This could suggest that the so-called cravings are not as different from any other motivationally efficacious desire (cf. Foddy and Savulescu 2006, 2010). Following this line of thought, addiction-motivated behavior could be reconsidered as a standard case of fully responsible agency, that is, intentional agency in the strong sense of having a plan rather than merely having a goal (Bratman 1984). But if so, we reach the opposite conclusion: being motivated by an addiction may sometimes constitute an aggravating rather an extenuating circumstance (Watson 1999; Morse 2000). That is to say, subjective irresistibility may be construed, on the one hand, as an excuse, if not a complete exemption from negative moral appraisal and on the other, as the result of willful—and reprehensible—self-indulgence.

This upshot leads us to the second kind of puzzles about addiction, which centers on the idea that addiction cannot be but wrong. In other words, should addiction-motivated behavior turn out to be a legitimate object for moral appraisal, this appraisal would necessarily take a negative form, in terms of blame and resentment. Alternatively, if addiction-motivated behavior falls outside the domain of responsible agency, it would still represent a wrong, more specifically, a blameless wrongdoing. Yet, the wrongness of addiction proves difficult to pin down. For instance, looking at Wallace (1994) it might be tempting to think that the wrongness of addiction is just a side effect of the kind of examples discussed: breaches of obligations in the context of addiction. However, such a conclusion would seem premature. Wallace (1994) makes a good case for the claim that addiction in general is likely to lead to disengagement from one's obligations. This claim is also supported by recent empirical studies and some first-personal memoirs of addiction (e.g. De Quincey 2002; Wurtzel 2002; Poland and Graham 2011). The point that these very different kinds of literature seem to concur on is that addiction, by its very nature, tends to override normative considerations that would otherwise be seen as compelling—by others who find themselves in a similar situation or even by the agent with addiction at an earlier stage when addiction has not yet taken hold of her life. Even so, a crucial puzzle about the wrongness of addiction remains unaddressed: Could this wrongness be, at least in principle, captured from within the third-personal perspective of an informed and impassive observer, such as Mr. Astley commenting on the Gambler's downfall (Dostoevsky 2008)? Alternatively, should the first-personal perspective of an agent with addiction be considered as indispensable when deciding whether a breach of obligation has even taken place? Compelling reasons speak in favor of both options. The very fact that normative issues about addiction-motivated behavior are exclusively focused on whether it may, in some circumstances, be worthy of excuse or exemption indicates that an addict's own evaluative perspective is taken to be tangential for the purposes of her moral appraisal. In other words, there seems to be an almost overwhelming assumption in favor of treating addictions as disordered appetites (Watson 2004) rather than strong idiosyncratic desires. And yet, as Watson (1999, p. 610) points out in the context of criminal responsibility: "the criminal law can be legitimate only if it is justifiable to those who are subjected to its demands. And it can meet the condition only if its subjects have reason to comply. The recognition of the space of agent-centered prerogatives, I suggest, is the law's acknowledgement of its own moral jurisdiction."

This conclusion holds true for responsibility in general and moral responsibility in particular. As we have seen in the earlier discussion (especially Chapter 2, Section 2.4), blame and resentment are reactive attitudes that are appropriately addressed only to full members of the moral community. But to be treated as a full member of the moral community means to have one's evaluative standpoint considered as equally significant as the standpoint that warrants one's negative moral appraisal. That is to say, blame and resentment are only fitting when they are addressed in a way that does not preclude, but on the contrary facilitates the expression of counter-justification, showing that blame and resentment were in fact unwarranted to start off with. This open-endedness is a distinctive feature of reactive attitudes as opposed to objective ones: reactive attitudes, such as resentment convey negative moral appraisal in order to re-engage the person that they are leveled at as a member of moral community. In this respect, negative moral appraisal validates a person's moral standing just as much, of not stronger than positive moral appraisal. This, however, is not the case with objective attitudes, the point of which is to solve a problem, to place a distance between ourselves and a source of threat, such as the human-feasting Satanists from Montmarquet's vignette (see Chapter 1, Section 1.4). To recap, the negative moral appraisal that almost uniformly attaches to addiction does not exhibit the kind of open-endedness that distinguishes reactive from objective attitudes. And yet, the fact that, like Mr. Astley's invective it is often addressed to the addicts themselves sits uncomfortably with the hypothesis that addicts have by default been confined to the margins of the moral community.

Attempts to give priority to the first-personal stance of an agent with addiction are marred with similar difficulties. For instance, Frankfurt's influential account of addiction (Chapter 1, Section 1.3) clearly posits that addiction becomes a problem of responsible agency only in so far as it is perceived as a problem by the addicted agent herself. On this view, a Happy Addict who endorses her addiction and the way that it shapes her life and actions is deemed as fit for success in action as an agent who gives due weight to the various normative considerations that the Happy Addict is bound to neglect. This outcome is counterintuitive: the fact that by the end of the novel the Gambler, to return to Dostoevsky's memorable work, eventually loses sight of what really matters and instead is fully absorbed by the vicissitudes of playing roulette looks like a worst kind of defeat, definitely not an exemplar of success in action. What on Frankfurtian terms counts as Happy Addiction clearly leads to less than successful agency to a considerably greater degree than Unhappy Addiction in the earlier period when the Gambler is still plagued by guilt for neglecting his intellectual pursuits and the company of his loved one. Once we begin to consider the addicts' own evaluative stance in earnest, we make a puzzling discovery: the apparent analogue of wholehearted commitment to one's pursuits, which is typically associated with success in action, in the context of addiction bodes—on the contrary—ultimate defeat in action. In light of the actualization model developed in this chapter, we are in a position to see that this is the central paradox, from which derive both kinds of puzzles considered earlier: whether addiction is compatible with intentional agency and how to account for the apparent wrongness of addiction.

The realization that this is the central paradox of addiction has an immediate payoff. It explains why subjective irresistibility of a course of action that an agent contemplates prompts two radically opposite conceptualizations depending on whether addiction is present or not: compulsion in the one instance, moral incapacity, volitional necessity, or practical identity in the other (Williams 1995; Korsgaard 1996; Frankfurt 1998; see Chapter 3, Section 3.3). Compulsion is a threat to intentional agency. It affects not only the ability to act in light of reasons but also its less visible counterpart, the ability to partake in shaping the space of valid reasons by engaging with the moral community from within. By contrast, moral incapacity and cognates are instances of subjective irresistibility that flow from an agent's well-attuned evaluative stance, that is, from the fact that she is a competent and mature valuer whose intentions are well-integrated instead of being conflicted in a way that makes success in action all but impossible for her.

These observations bring into relief the interest of explaining addiction in terms of akrasia, on the Aristotelian view fleshed out in the course of this inquiry. For, this view is able not only to account for the various puzzles raised by the phenomenology of addiction, but also to provide us with a cogent normative framework avoiding the unsatisfactory dichotomy of a medical versus a criminal model of responsibility for addiction. The conclusions supported by the argument of this book can be summarized as follows:

(1) Like weakness of will, addiction is a secondary failure of intentional agency, which derives from akrasia, a primary failure of intentional agency that makes all relevant actions necessarily less than successful. For an akratic action is defined by a structural tension between success as production and success as assertion. This structural tension becomes apparent when we apply to akrasia the general model of responsible or morally relevant action proposed here—action as actualization.

(2) Unlike weakness of will, addiction is associated with a sense of compulsion rather than merely giving in to some guilty pleasure or other. The contrast is frequently posited in recent philosophical works on weakness of will. However, no positive account has been offered as to why we should distinguish the two phenomena in this way, though of course skeptics about weakness of will have presented arguments for the insignificance of this contrast and proponents have aimed to refute these arguments (Radoilska 2013b). Applied to addiction and weakness of will, the actualization model provides such a positive account. Weak-willed pursuits depend on being perceived as pleasurable, albeit unworthy. Once a weak-willed agent experiences these pursuits as fundamentally disappointing sources of pleasure,

she also grows out of her weakness of will. By contrast, addictive behavior transcends the experience of pleasure initially associated with the object of addiction. As illustrated by De Quincey (2002) and Dostoevsky (2008), addiction is bound to survive addicts' recurrent experience of their addictions as harmful, distressing, and painful. In this respect, addiction is not just a recalcitrant form of akrasia, which is essentially true of weakness of will, but more importantly a form of akrasia that is utterly devoid of pleasure. Paradoxically, or ironically, being devoid of pleasure is what makes addiction compulsive: the pursuit of a specter of pleasure is bound to be insatiable. In this sense, addiction could be said to involve a disoriented, if not a disordered appetite.

(3) The difference between weakness of will and addiction is not one of degree, but of kind. Looking again at De Quincey (2002) and Dostoevsky (2008), the pleasure that could be derived from the object of future addiction is already blown out of proportion before the onset of addiction and even before any actual first-hand experience of this object. And so, addiction arguably presents a more radical category of less than successful agency than weakness of will: addictive behavior aims at success in action at the expense of action.

(4) The main implication of the proposed analysis with respect to responsibility for addiction is to assuage skepticism about the use of evaluative and especially ethical vocabulary in this context. For instance, some authors aim to avoid framing problems of addiction in explicitly evaluative terms since they consider that this would further stigmatize people with addiction. In light of the preceding discussion, we can appreciate why such a strategy would be necessarily counterproductive; it would feed into the objectifying attitudes implicit in the two partial models of responsible action—action as production and action as assertion—that make both volitional and non-volitional accounts of addiction ultimately disappointing. In contrast, negative moral appraisal strengthens the person with addiction by reengaging with her as an apt valuer that could also act under the guise of

the good, not only the apparent—and disappearing—good of her addiction. For, as argued throughout this work, evaluative immaturity is what necessarily leads to less than successful pursuits, such as akrasia, weakness of will, and addiction. At the same time, however, evaluative immaturity is always object- or pursuit-centered rather than global: less than successful agency still takes place under the guise of the good. And so success in action is never completely out of sight.

References

Ainslie, G. (2001). *Breakdown of Will*. Cambridge: Cambridge University Press.

Aristotle (1984). *The Complete Works of Aristotle* (ed. J. Barnes). Vols. 1 and 2. Princeton, NJ: Princeton University Press.

American Psychiatric Association (2001). *DSM-IV-TR: Diagnostic and Statistical Manual of Mental Disorders*, 4th ed. (text rev.). Washington, DC: American Psychiatric Association.

Anscombe, G.E.M. (1958). Modern moral philosophy. *Journal of Philosophy* **33**: 1–19.

Anscombe, G.E.M. (1963). *Intention*, 2nd ed. Oxford: Blackwell.

Arpaly, N. (2003). *Unprincipled Virtue: An Inquiry into Moral Agency*. Oxford: Oxford University Press.

Arpaly, N. (2006). *Merit, Meaning, and Human Bondage*. Princeton, NJ: Princeton University Press.

Arpaly, N. and Schroeder, T. (1999). Praise, blame, and the whole self. *Philosophical Studies* **93**: 161–188.

Audi, R. (1979). Weakness of will and practical judgment. *Noûs* **13**: 173–196.

Berridge, K. and Robinson, T. (2011). Drug addiction and incentive sensitization. In J. Poland and G. Graham (eds.), *Addiction and Responsibility*. Cambridge, MA: MIT Press; 21–53.

Bobonich, C. and Destrée, P. (eds.) (2007). *Akrasia in Greek Philosophy: From Socrates to Plotinus*. Leiden: E.J. Brill.

Bratman, M. (1984). Two faces of intention. *Philosophical Review* **93**: 375–405.

Bratman, M. (1987). *Intention, Plans and Practical Reason*. Cambridge, MA: Harvard University Press.

Bratman, M. (2007). *Structures of Agency*. Oxford: Oxford University Press.

Broadie, S. (1994). Another problem of akrasia. *International Journal of Philosophical Studies* **2**: 229–242.

Burnyeat, M. (1980). Aristotle on learning to be good. In A.O. Rorty (ed.), *Essays on Aristotle's Ethics*. Berkeley, CA: University of California Press; 68–92.

Buss, S. and Overton, L. (2002). *Contours of Agency: Essays on Themes from Harry Frankfurt*. Cambridge, MA: MIT Press.

Canto-Sperber, M. (2001). Movements des animaux et motivation himaine dans le livre III du De Anima d'Aristote. In M. Canto-Sperber, *Ethiques Grecques*. Paris: Presses Universitaires de France; 263–322.

Catullus, G.V. (1990). *The Poems of Catullus* (transl. G. Lee). Oxford: Clarendon Press.

Charles, D. (1984). *Aristotle's Philosophy of Action*. London: Duckworth.

Charles, D. (2009). Nicomachean Ethics 7.3: varieties of akrasia. In C. Natali (ed.), *Aristotle: Nicomachean Ethics Book VII: Symposium Aristotelicum*. Oxford: Oxford University Press; 41–71.

Corcilius, K. (2008a). Two jobs for Aristotle's practical syllogism? *Logical Analysis and History of Philosophy* 11: 163–184.

Corcilius, K. (2008b). Aristoteles' praktishe Syllogismen in der zweiten Hälfte des 20. Jahrhunderts. *Logical Analysis and History of Philosophy* 11: 101–132.

Davidson, D. (2001). How is weakness of the will possible? In D. Davidison, *Essays on Actions and Events*. Oxford: Clarendon Press; 21–42.

Davidson, D. (2004). Paradoxes of irrationality. In D. Davidson, *Problems of Rationality*. Oxford: Oxford University Press; 170–188.

De Quincey, T. (2002). *Confessions of an English Opium-Eater*. Otley: Woodstock.

Destrée, P. (2007). Aristotle on the causes of akrasia. In C. Bobonich and P. Destrée (eds.), *Akrasia in Greek Philosophy: From Socrates to Plotinus*. Leiden: Brill; 139–165.

Dostoevsky, F. (2008). The Gambler. In F. Dostoevsky, *Notes from the Underground* and *The Gambler* (transl. J. Kentish). Oxford: Oxford University Press; 125–284.

Elster, J. (1984). *Ulysses and the Sirens: Studies in Rationality and Irrationality*. Cambridge: Cambridge University Press.

Elster, J. (ed.) (1999). *Addiction: Entries and Exits*. New York: Russel Sage.

Elster, J. (2000). *Ulysses Unbound: Studies in Rationality, Precommitment, and Constraints*. Cambridge: Cambridge University Press.

Fisher, J.M. (2003). Responsibility and alternative possibilities. In D. Widerker and McKenna, M. (eds.), *Moral Responsibility and Alternative Possibilities: Essays on the Importance of Alternative Possibilities*. Aldershot: Ashgate; 27–52.

Flatauer, S. (transl. from German) (1981). *Autobiography of a Child Prostitute and Heroin Addict: Christiane F.* London: Arlington Books.

Foddy, B. and Savulescu, J. (2006). Addiction and autonomy: can addicted people consent to the prescription of their drug of addiction? *Bioethics* 20: 1–15.

Foddy, B. and Savulescu, J. (2010). A liberal account of addiction. *Philosophy, Psychiatry & Psychology* 17: 1–22.

Foot, P. (1995). Does moral subjectivism rest on a mistake? *Oxford Journal of Legal Studies* 15: 1–14.

Frankfurt, H. (1969). Alternate possibilities and moral responsibility. *Journal of Philosophy* 66: 829–839.

Frankfurt, H. (1971). Freedom of the will and the concept of a person. *Journal of Philosophy* 68: 5–20.

Frankfurt, H. (1989). Concerning the freedom and limits of the will. *Philosophical Topics* 17: 119–130.

Frankfurt, H. (1998). *The Importance of What We Care About*. Cambridge: Cambridge University Press.

Frede, D. (2006). Pleasure and pain in Aristotle's Ethics. In R. Kraut (ed.), *The Blackwell Guide to Aristotle's Nicomachean Ethics*. Oxford: Blackwell; 255–275.

Furley, D. (1980). Self-movers. In A.O. Rorty, (ed.), *Essays on Aristotle's Ethics*, Berkeley, CA: University of California Press; 55–67.

Garcia, J.L.A. (1990). The intentional and the intended. *Erkenntnis* 33: 191–209.

Garner, A. and Hardcastle, V.G. (2004). Neurobiological models: an unnecessary divide—neural models in psychiatry. In J. Radden (ed.), *The Philosophy of Psychiatry: A Companion*. New York: Oxford University Press; 364–380.

Grgic, F. (2002). Aristotle on the akratic's knowledge. *Phronesis* 47: 337–338.

Hare, R. (1952). *The Language of Moral*. Oxford: Clarendon Press.

Harris, V. (2012). Intoxicating trends. *History Today* 62(4).

Hart, H.L.A. (1961). *The Concept of Law*. Oxford: Clarendon Press.

Hieronymi, P. (2008). Responsibility for believing. *Synthese* **161**: 357–373.

Hieronymi, P. (2009). Believing at will. *Canadian Journal of Philosophy* 35(Suppl.): 149–187.

Holton, R. (1999). Intention and weakness of will. *Journal of Philosophy* 96: 241–262.

Holton, R. (2003). How is strength of will possible? In S. Stroud and C. Tappolet (eds.), *Weakness of Will and Practical Rationality*. Oxford: Clarendon Press; 39–67.

Holton, R. (2009). *Willing, Wanting, Waiting*. Oxford: Oxford University Press.

Jackson, F. (1998). *From Metaphysics to Ethics*. Oxford: Oxford University Press.

Kant, I. (1996a). Critique of Practical Reason. In I. Kant. *Practical Philosophy* (transl. M.G. Gregor). Cambridge: Cambridge University Press; 133–271.

Kant, I. (1996b). Groundwork of The Metaphysics of Morals. In I. Kant, *Practical Philosophy* (transl. M.G. Gregor). Cambridge: Cambridge University Press; 37–108.

Kim, J. (1993). *Supervenience and Mind: Selected Philosophical Essays*. Cambridge: Cambridge University Press.

Korsgaard, C.M. (1996). *Sources of Normativity*. Cambridge: Cambridge University Press.

Korsgaard, C.M. (2008). *The Constitution of Agency: Essays on Practical Reason and Moral Psychology*. Oxford: Oxford University Press.

Labarrière, J.-L. (1984). Imagination humaine et imagination animale chez Aristote. *Phronesis* **29**: 17–49.

Labarrière, J.-L. (1990). De la phronèsis animale. In D. Devereux and P. Pellegrin (eds.), *Biologie, logique et métaphysique chez Aristote*. Paris: Éd. du CNRS; 405–428.

Lear, G.R. (2006). Aristotle on moral virtue and the fine. In R. Kraut (ed.), *The Blackwell Guide to Aristotle's Nicomachean Ethics*. Oxford: Blackwell; 116–136.

Levy, N. (2005). The good, the bad, and the blameworthy. *Journal of Ethics and Social Philosophy* **1**: 1–16.

Levy, N. (2006). Autonomy and addiction. *Canadian Journal of Philosophy* **36**: 427–448.

Levy, N. (2011). Addiction, responsibility, and ego depletion. In J. Poland and G. Graham (eds.), *Addiction and Responsibility*. Cambridge, MA: MIT Press; 89–111.

MacIntyre, A. (2008). Conflicts of desire. In T. Hoffmann (ed.), *Weakness of Will from Plato to the Present*. Washington, DC: The Catholic University of America Press; 276–292.

Mele, A.R. (1987). *Irrationality: An Essay of Akrasia, Self-Deception, and Self-Control*. New York: Oxford University Press.

Mele, A.R. (1995). *Autonomous Agents: from Self-Control to Autonomy*. New York: Oxford University Press.

Mele, A.R. (2002). Akratics and addicts. *American Philosophical Quarterly* **39**: 153–167.

Mele, A.R. (2010). Weakness of will and akrasia. *Philosophical Studies* **150**: 391–404.

Mele, A.R. (2012). *Backsliding: Understanding Weakness of Will*. Oxford: Oxford University Press.

Mishima, Y. (2001). *The Temple of the Golden Pavilion* (transl. I. Morris). London: Vintage.

Montmarquet, J. (2002). Wallace's "Kantian" Strawsonianism. *Philosophy and Phenomenological Research* **64**: 687–692.

Morse, S. (2000). Hooked on hype: addiction and responsibility. *Law and Philosophy* **19**: 3–49.

Nussbaum, M.C. (1979). *Aristotle's De Motu Animalium: Text with Translation, Commentary and Interpretative Essays*. Princeton, NJ: Princeton University Press.

Pears, D.F. and Pugmire, D. (1982). Motivated irrationality. *Proceedings of the Aristotelian Society* **56**: 157–196.

Pickavé, M. and Whiting, J. (2008). Nicomachean Ethics 7.3 on akratic ignorance. *Oxford Studies in Ancient Philosophy* **34**: 323–371.

Poland, J. and Graham, G. (eds.) (2011). *Addiction and Responsibility*. Cambridge, MA: MIT Press.

Plato (1992). *Republic*, 2nd ed. (transl. G.M.A. Grube). Indianapolis, IN: Hackett Publishing Company.

Plato (2008). *Protagoras*. (transl. N. Denyer). Cambridge: Cambridge University Press.

Radoilska, L. (2007). *L'actualité d'Aristote en morale*. Paris: Presses Universitaires de France.

Radoilska, L. (2010). An Aristotelian approach to cognitive enhancement. *Journal of Value Inquiry* **44**: 365–375.

Radoilska, L. (2012a). Autonomy and Ulysses arrangements. In L. Radoilska (ed.), *Autonomy and Mental Disorder*. Oxford: Oxford University Press; 252–280.

Radoilska, L. (2012b). Personal autonomy, decisional capacity, and mental disorder. In L. Radoilska (ed.), *Autonomy and Mental Disorder*. Oxford: Oxford University Press, xi–xliii.

Radoilska, L. (2012c). Akrasia and ordinary weakness of will. *Tópicos* **43**: 26–50.

Radoilska, L. (2013a). Depression, decisional capacity, and personal autonomy. In K.W.M. Fulford, M. Davies, R. Gipps, G. Graham, J. Sadler, G. Stanghellini, and T. Thornton (eds.), *The Oxford Handbook of Philosophy and Psychiatry*. Oxford: Oxford University Press; 1155–1170.

Radoilska, L. (2013b). Weakness of will. In D. Pritchard (ed.), *Oxford Bibliographies Online: Philosophy*. <http://www.oxfordbibliographies.com/>

Raz, J. (2011). *From Normativity to Responsibility*. New York: Oxford University Press.

Ricoeur, P. (1990). *Soi-même comme un autre*. Paris: Seuil.

Rogers, K. (1999). Aristotle's conception of τὸ καλόν. In L. Gerson (ed.), *Aristotle: Critical Assessments*. London: Routledge; 337–355.

Sartre, J.-P. (2003). *Being and Nothingness: an Essay on Phenomenological Ontology* (transl. H.E. Barnes). London: Routledge.

Sartre, J.-P. (2007). *Existentialism is a Humanism* (transl. C. Macomber). New Haven, CT: Yale University Press.

Scanlon, T. (2008). *Moral Dimensions: Permissibility, Meaning, Blame*. Cambridge, MA: Belknap Press.

Sellman, D. (2009). The 10 most important things known about addiction. *Addiction* **105**: 6–13.

Shapiro, T. (2001). Three conceptions of action in moral theory. *Noûs* **35**: 93–117.

Shoemaker, D. (2009). Responsibility and disability. *Metaphilosophy* **40**: 438–461.

Shoemaker, D. (2011). Attributability, answerability, and accountability: toward a wider theory of moral responsibility. *Ethics* **121**: 603–632.

Smart, J.J.C. (1961). Free will, praise, and blame. *Mind* **70**: 291–306.

Smith, A. (2005). Responsibility for attitudes: activity and passivity in mental life. *Ethics* **115**: 236–271.

Smith, A. (2008). Control, responsibility, and moral assessment. *Philosophical Studies* **138**: 367–392.

Smith, A. (2012). Attributability, answerability, and accountability: in defense of a unified account. *Ethics* **122**: 575–589.

Solomon, A. (1998). Anatomy of melancholy. *The New Yorker* 12 January: 46–61.

Sophocles (2001). *Philoctetes* (trans. J. Affleck). Cambridge: Cambridge University Press.

Sophocles (2004). *Antigone* (transl. S. Heaney). London: Faber.

Southwood, N. (2011). The moral/convention distinction. *Mind* **120**: 761–802.

Stocker, M. (1979). Desiring the bad: an essay in moral psychology. *Journal of Philosophy* **76**: 738–753.

Strawson, P. (1962). Freedom and resentment. *Proceedings of the British Academy* **48**:1–25.

Suikkanen, J. (2011). Intentions, blame, and contractualism. A critical review of T.M. Scanlon's Moral Dimensions: Permissibility, Meaning, Blame. *Jurisprudence* **2**: 561–573.

Tenenbaum, S. (2007). *Appearances of the Good: An Essay on the Nature of Practical Reason*. New York: Cambridge University Press.

Velleman, D. (1992). The Guise of the Good. *Noûs* **26**: 3–26.

Wallace, R.J. (1994). *Responsibility and the Moral Sentiments*. Cambridge, MA: Harvard Universtity Press.

Wallace, R.J. (1999). Addiction as defect of the will: some philosophical reflections. *Law and Philosophy* **18**: 621–654.

Wallace, R.J. (2001). Normativity, commitment, and instrumental reason. *Philosophers' Imprint* **1**: 1–26.

Wallace, R.J. (2002a). Précis of responsibility and the moral sentiments. *Philosophy and Phenomenological Research* **64(3)**: 680–681.

Wallace, R.J. (2002b). Replies. *Philosophy and Phenomenological Research* **64**: 707–727.

Watson, G. (1977). Scepticism about weakness of will. *Philosophical Review* **86**: 316–339.

Watson, G. (1996). Two faces of responsibility. *Philosophical Topics* **24**: 227–248.

Watson, G. (1999). Excusing addiction. *Law and Philosophy* **18**: 589–619.

Watson, G. (2004). Disordered appetites: addiction, compulsion, and dependence. In G. Watson, *Agency and Answerability*. New York: Oxford University Press; 59–87.

Wedgwood, R. (2003). Choosing rationally and choosing correctly. In S. Stroud and C. Tappolet (eds.), *Weakness of Will and Practical Rationality*. Oxford: Clarendon Press; 201–229.

Widerker, D. (2003). Blameworthiness and Frankfurt's arguments against the principle of alternative possibilities. In D. Widerker and M. McKenna (eds.), *Moral Responsibility and Alternative Possibilities: Essays on the Importance of Alternative Possibilities*. Aldershot: Ashgate; 53–73.

Widerker, D. and McKenna, M. (eds.) (2003). *Moral Responsibility and Alternative Possibilities: Essays on the Importance of Alternative Possibilities*. Aldershot: Ashgate.

Wiggins, D. (1979). Weakness of will, commensurability, and the objects of deliberation and desire. *Proceedings of the Aristotelian Society* **79**: 251–277.

Wiggins, D. (1998). Truth, invention, and the meaning of life. In D. Wiggins, *Needs, Values, and Truth*, 3rd ed. Oxford: Oxford University Press, 87–138.

Williams, B. (1981). Internal and external reasons. In B. Williams, *Moral Luck*. Cambridge: Cambridge University Press; 101–113.

Williams, B. (1995). Moral incapacity. In B. Williams, *Making Sense of Humanity*. Cambridge: Cambridge University Press; 46–55.

World Health Organization (1992). *The ICD-10 Classification of Mental and Behavioural Disorders*. Geneva: World Health Organization.

Wurtzel, E. (2002). *More, Now, Again: A Memoir of Addiction*. New York: Simon & Schuster.

Index